Kimono
きもの
日本語 Level 1

Chief writer and coordinator:
Helen McBride

Illustrated by
Bettina Guthridge
Designed by
Josie Semmler

Contributing writers
Michael Sedunary
Yukiko Saegusa
Sue Burnham
Christine Poulter
Peter Williams
Elio Guarnuccio

Consultants
Hisako Yoshiki
Masako Hamahashi
Kazuko Eguchi
Monica Pinda
Glenn Taylor

CIS Educational

Heinemann

HARCOURT EDUCATION

22 Salmon Street, Port Melbourne, Victoria 3207
World Wide Web hi.com.au
Email info@hi.com.au

© Michael Sedunary 1990
First published by CIS Educational 1990
2009 2008 2007 2006 2005
20 19 18 17 16 15 14

Edited by Helen McBride
Illustrated by Bettina Guthridge
Designed and typeset by Josie Semmler

Film supplied by Typescan, Adelaide
Printed in China by WKT

National Library of Australia cataloguing-in-publication data:

McBride, Helen.
  Kimono.
  ISBN 0 94991 966 7.

  1. Japanese language – Textbooks for foreign speakers – English.
  I. Guthridge, Bettina. II. Title.

495.682421

Reed International Books Australia Pty Ltd

ACN 001 002 357

Contents ・ もくじ

きもの 1
おはよう!

Communicative tasks
Greetings
Saying goodbye
Saying your name
Apologising
Expressing surprise

Situations and vocabulary
Greetings
Numbers: 一 二 三 四 五 六

Language points
When and where to use the greetings
Using titles with other people's names: さん, くん, せんせい

Cultural and linguistic background
Greetings and bowing
日本 - introduction to Japan and its position relative to the rest of the world
Introduction to Japanese writing systems

きもの 2
おなまえは?

Communicative tasks
Meeting people
More on asking and saying your name
Asking and saying how old you are
Saying thank you
Asking and saying how to say a word in Japanese

Situations and vocabulary
Some classroom items
Numbers: 七 - 十三

Language points
…です
…ですか
なんさい ですか
十二/十三さい です
なん ですか

Cultural and linguistic background
日本に いきましょう! - preparing to visit Japan
日本語の はつおん - the importance of getting your pronunciation right
うた - Kotsu kotsu

ひらがな 一

Introduction to reading and writing ひらがな

きもの 6
どう した ん
です か

Communicative tasks
Talking about what you did at
the weekend
Talking about what other
people did
Telling the time on the hour
and half-hour

Situations and vocabulary
Leisure activities
Sports
Days of the week

Language points
Time words + に
...を...ました
なんじ です か
...じ(はん)です
...よ

*Cultural and linguistic
background*
A day shopping in Tokyo
わかりましたか - Listening
skills

きもの 7
たのしかった
です よ

Communicative tasks
More on talking about what
you did
Talking about where
you went
Commenting on what something
was like
Identifying family members

Situations and vocabulary
Time words: せんしゅう,
きのう
Places to go
Members of the family

Language points
...に...ました
どう でしたか
...かった です よ

*Cultural and linguistic
background*
School excursion to Kyoto and
Nara - leaving Tokyo on the
しんかんせん
Let's be flexible - being open
to other ways of expressing
things

きもの 8
いって らっしゃい!

Communicative tasks
Talking about what you are
going to do
Making suggestions to do
something
Asking and saying at what
time you do something

Situations and vocabulary
More leisure activities
More time words: あした,
らいしゅう, らいねん
Modes of transport

Language points
...ましょう
...ますか
なんじに...
...と...
で meaning *by*
More on に

*Cultural and linguistic
background*
School excursion to Kyoto
and Nara - visiting the ancient
capitals of Japan

きもの is the first level of a communicative Japanese course for young students. It takes a lively, humorous approach to the teaching of Japanese. From the point of view of method, it is comprehensive rather than exclusive, seeking to combine the best of current language teaching theory in a commonsense, practical resource book which has appeal for both students and teachers.

At this beginner's stage, students are introduced to the Japanese language and culture in a context which is relevant to their own interests and experience. Thus, students learn the language required to talk about themselves, their school environment, their family, sport, leisure, food and drink.

Full-colour まんが, illustrations and photography are designed to stimulate interest and participation in a series of imaginative activities. These activities are supported by carefully graded and clearly worded grammatical explanations. In this way students are offered a large amount of communicative language, underpinned by a systematic study of the structure of the language, thus catering for a range of learning and teaching styles.

The Japanese script

In きもの Level 1 students learn to read and write *hiragana* and recognise some *kanji*. Right from unit 1 all Japanese is written in *hiragana*. *Roomaji* is only used for *katakana* words as *katakana* is not introduced until きもの Level 2.

Thus, as far as possible at this beginner's stage, きもの presents the Japanese language and writing systems as a whole. As a result there is no danger that students can come to regard writing as an adjunct to the language rather than an integral part.

Hiragana is introduced in two intensive units, ひらがな一 and 二, which come after units 2 and 4. What are basically presentation units in the textbook, are supported by extensive practice in the *Workbook*. Therefore in units 1 and 2, where students have not yet been introduced to the script, the emphasis is on recognising the *hiragana* symbols and learning simple language through listening and imitating. However, the book has been designed so that ひらがな一 and 二 stand alone, giving teachers the choice of teaching *hiragana* even before starting unit 1 if they wish.

きもの textbook

The きもの textbook comprises the following elements:

まんが

The full-colour まんが at the start of each unit encapsulates the language taught in the whole unit in a stimulating and challenging way. Enjoyment of and response to these cartoons can lead on to pronunciation practice, comprehension activities, role-playing, adaptation and creation of original stories.

いいましょう

The いいましょう exercises provide visual information which brings into focus a particular language point for intensive oral practice. Since they isolate and highlight the important language points in each unit and introduce new vocabulary, some teachers may prefer to use the いいましょう exercises as a way of introducing the work in the unit before tackling the まんが.

The いいましょう exercises in きもの are designed primarily to be done with the whole class. Since many of these exercises introduce new vocabulary, in most cases a period of preparation, in which students become familiar with the new words, will be required before chorussed responses can be achieved. Ideas for exploiting these いいましょう exercises are contained in the *Teacher's Manual*.

きいて いいましょう

The きいて いいましょう exercises occur in the first three units of きもの, while students are coming to terms with *hiragana*. In these exercises students have to respond to aural stimuli such as sounds, stabs of music and verbal clues and associate them with pictures.

ともだちと

From unit 4, きいて いいましょう section is replaced by ともだちと. These pair-work exercises are a stage along the way towards unstructured conversation. Students have to make a series of sensible choices of phrases in context in order to build up a coherent dialogue.

いきいきと はなしましょう

This is the most challenging oral activity in each unit. Students are given a communicative task in a realistic situation which gives them scope to make creative use of the language they have been learning. This is really the critical point in each unit, the point to which the preceding language exercises and activities have been leading.

日本語 nooto

The role of this section is to provide a simple, clear synthesis of the language covered in each unit. It is not intended as a starting point, being deliberately placed after the main language section of the unit as a summary of what has already been covered. The aim is to pick up and systematise certain points in a straightforward and helpful way. Language points are only explained within the scope of the unit or build on what students already know.

せいかつ

The study of Japanese culture is an integral part of the きもの course. It aims to stimulate students' interest in Japan by looking at those aspects of Japanese culture which are relevant and interesting to the age group. In addition to basic geographical and historical information about Japan, students are given a view of contemporary Japanese life through a series of letters written by a thirteen year old foreign girl staying with a Japanese family in Japan. Full-colour photographs supporting each cultural section provide an important visual aspect to the written information.

Exercises, activities and ideas for follow-up projects based on these topics are contained in the きもの *Workbook* and *Teacher's Manual*.

がんばれ!

Most units of きもの contain a がんばれ section. This section aims to give students general strategies for effective language learning and show how they can be applied to Japanese.

Through this section, students are also given some insights into the relationship between different languages and language and culture.

たんご

Each unit contains a summary of vocabulary introduced in the unit. Wherever possible, a variety of presentations has been used to avoid intimidating lists of words and expressions.

Many times the いいましょう pages act as a たんご by presenting new vocabulary through photographs or illustrations. In any case, new vocabulary is always divided into categories to make the task of learning vocabulary a more manageable one. All vocabulary lists are arranged in the order of the Japanese syllabary chart.

At the end of the book there is a reference page of numbers and the numeral classifiers covered in the book. This is followed by a complete 日本語ー英語, 英語ー日本語 vocabulary listing.

おめでとう!

At the end of each unit is a summary of what the students can do in Japanese as a result of completing the unit.

きもの Workbook

The *Workbook* accompanying the きもの textbook is a vital component of the course. It contains a wide variety of exercise and activity types designed to exploit the material presented in the text and provides a thorough consolidation of the language points raised. The *Workbook* contains the following elements:

ききましょう - Listening comprehension exercises, the texts of which are recorded on the きもの cassettes and reproduced in the *Teacher's Manual*.

れんしゅう しましょう - The main 'body' of each *Workbook* unit. This section contains a wide range of exercises and activities to provide mainly written reinforcement of the language content of each unit.

日本に ついて - Exercises and activities exploiting the cultural material in each unit.

きもの Teacher's Manual

An invaluable resource for the teacher, this manual includes the following elements:

The きもの method - An expanded discussion of points touched on in this introduction.

Teacher's notes - How to use and exploit to the fullest all of the individual items in the course; how to use the course in class; sample lesson plans and guidelines for assessment.

Unit-by-unit analysis - Includes a summary of language presented, classroom expressions, content of cassettes, suggestions for presenting each いいましょう exercise, scripts of listening comprehension activities, ideas for games and cultural units.

Reproduction masters - Include reading comprehension passages, cartoon pages with separate listings of speech bubbles and student progress sheets.

きもの cassettes

For each unit of the course, the cassettes contain:

· An entertaining recording of the まんが, both at normal speed and with pauses for repetition.
· Listening comprehension activities.
· A presentation of each いいましょう exercise.
· Songs and other items of interest in Japanese.

Acknowledgements

The publishers wish to thank the following people who made a contribution in the preparation of this book:

· Mr Hamada and his staff at the Japanese Consulate-General
· Shohei Baba, Principal of the Hosei University First High School in Tokyo for his hospitality and assistance
· Mr H. Take and students of the Japan School in Melbourne for their assistance and cooperation
· Shozo Miura, for preparation of Japanese food on page 60
· Leo Sedunary for providing valuable insights into contemporary life in Japan
· Bill Farr and Ken Uchida for their general assistance

The publishers also wish to acknowledge the following people and organisations who supplied the photographs appearing in this book:

· International Society for Educational Information, Inc. for the photographs appearing on the following pages:
p 7, p 8 bottom right, p 9 right, p 15 (Kishimoto Corporation), p 21 left, p 39, p 50 bottom right, p 51, p 58 bottom left, p 77 kendo, baseball, volleyball, karate (Kishimoto Corporation), sumo wrestling (Nihon sumoo kyookai), p 78 bottom (Metropolitan Express Public Corporation), p 84, p 88, p 89
· Elio Guarnuccio, Josie Semmler, Sue Burnham, Helen Semmler, Giselle Bates, Anthony King and George Dale who supplied all other photographs

End-paper design taken from Clarence P. Hornung, *Allover Patterns for Designers and Craftsmen*, Dover Publications, Inc., New York

Finally, the publishers gratefully acknowledge the companies who kindly gave their permission to use copyright material in this book. Despite every effort, the publishers were not always successful in tracing all copyright owners. Should this come to the attention of the copyright owners concerned, the publishers request that they contact them so that proper acknowledgement can be made in any reprint of this book.

きもの 1 ・ おはよう!

いいましょう一

一	二	三	四	五
おはよう ございます	こんにちは	さようなら	こんばんは	おやすみ なさい

Say the greetings using the example as a guide.

例：

A みなさん、こんにちは。
B せんせい、こんにちは。

おはよう ございます。

一... 二... 三... 四... 五... 六...

Practise counting to six in Japanese.

いいましょう 二

おなまえは?

(一) ただしです。

(四) はるこです。

(二) ゆうこです。

(五) あきおです。

(三) としおです。

(六) みちこです。

Listen to these people giving their names. Practise giving your own name using the example as a guide.

例:

A	おなまえは?
B	ただしです。

きいて いいましょう

一 — Sounds are often a clue to the time of day and the greeting that you use. Listen to the sound on the tape and say the greeting that matches it in the pauses provided. Here is an example.

例:
おはよう ございます。

二 — You're at a big party and you notice that all the characters from きもの are there. You are dying to speak to them, so you try to get their attention. Listen to the example on the tape, then speak in the pauses provided.

例:
あっ! はなこさん!

いきいきと はなしましょう

一 Write your name and a time of day on a piece of paper, and put it in a hat along with everyone else's in the class.
e.g. Robin 2 p.m.
Now, in turn, pick out a name and go over and greet the person. Make sure your greeting matches the time shown.

二 In groups, record each member of the group saying a different greeting. Play it to the rest of the class. They must try and guess who is saying each greeting, for example, Biru くん です。

三 Try putting the Japanese words you know to music. Listen to the sample tune on the cassette, and see if you can make up your own song using the Japanese words you have learned so far. Those of you who are more musically minded may like to make up a tune as well.
一...二...三...

たんご

New words and expressions

あっ!? __ oh! ah!
えっ!? __ what's this!?
おなまえは? __ what's your name?
すみません __ I'm sorry, excuse me
せんせい __ teacher
です __ am, are, is
みなさん __ everyone
わあ! __ ahhh!

Numbers

一 __	one __	(いち)
二 __	two __	(に)
三 __	three __	(さん)
四 __	four __	(よん or し)
五 __	five __	(ご)
六 __	six __	(ろく)

Greetings

おはよう! __ morning!
おはよう ございます __ good morning
おやすみ なさい __ goodnight
こんにちは __ good afternoon/hello
こんばんは __ good evening
さようなら __ goodbye
じゃ またね __ see you later

じゃまたね。

日本

さっぽろ
(Sapporo)

**ほっかいどう
(HOKKAIDOO)**

Japan is a long narrow country. If you were to travel its whole length from north to south, you would travel approximately 3,700 kilometres. Look at the map and decide which way you would go.
What means of transport would you use?
What kind of journey would it be?

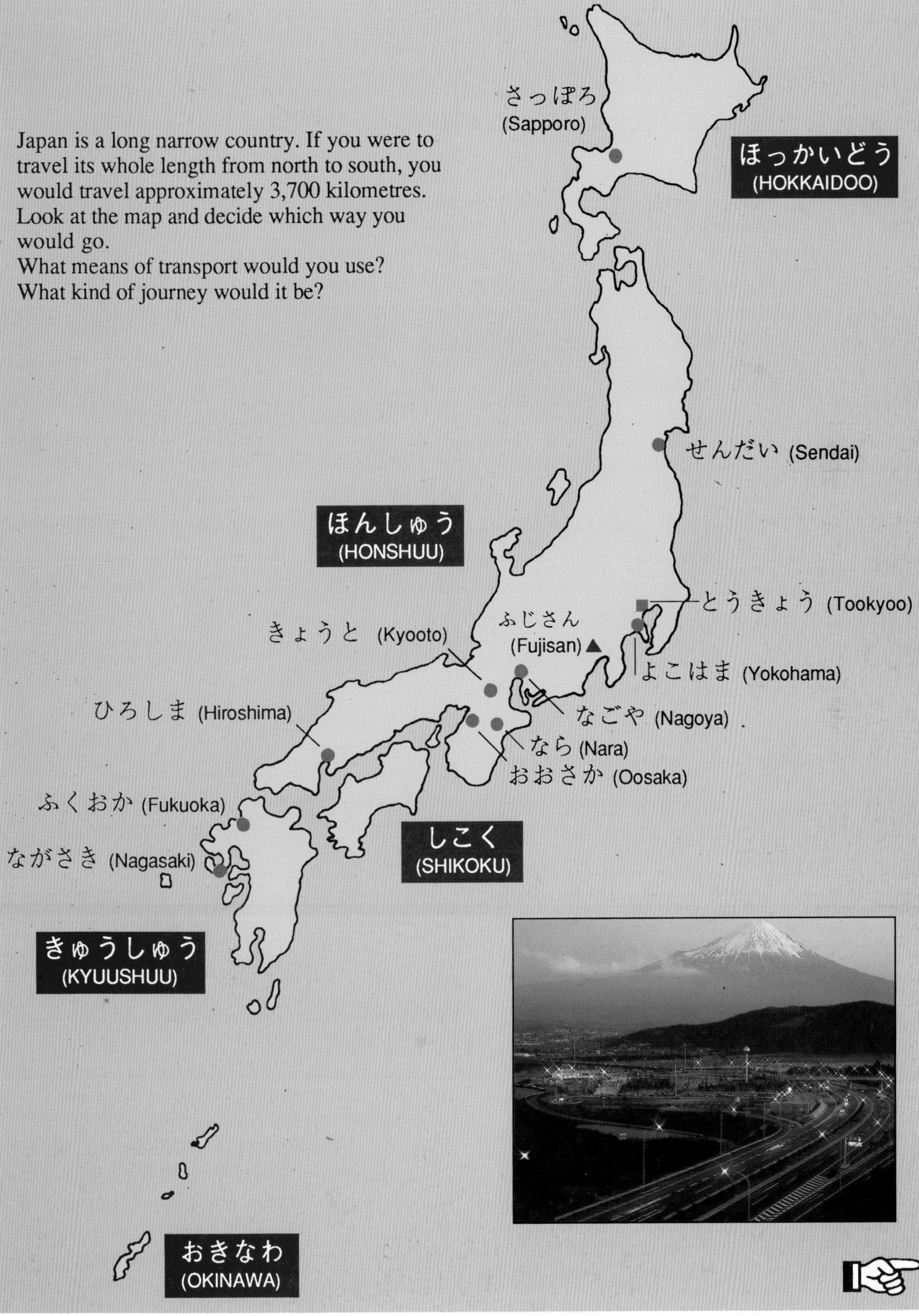

せんだい (Sendai)

**ほんしゅう
(HONSHUU)**

きょうと (Kyooto)

ふじさん
(Fujisan) ▲

とうきょう (Tookyoo)

よこはま (Yokohama)

ひろしま (Hiroshima)

なごや (Nagoya)

なら (Nara)

おおさか (Oosaka)

ふくおか (Fukuoka)

ながさき (Nagasaki)

**しこく
(SHIKOKU)**

**きゅうしゅう
(KYUUSHUU)**

**おきなわ
(OKINAWA)**

Well, for a start you would not be travelling always on land as Japan is a collection of islands. There would be many times when you would have to catch a ferry or cross a long bridge like this one. And if you were travelling by train, you would find yourself going through a long tunnel under the sea between the islands of ほっかいどう and ほんしゅう.

The Seto Bridge connects the islands of ほんしゅう and しこく

The largest and most well-known islands that make up Japan are ほっかいどう, ほんしゅう, しこく and きゅうしゅう. In addition, Japan includes almost 4,000 smaller islands scattered along the coast of these larger ones. So, if you wanted to, you could travel the whole length of Japan by boat, hopping from one island to another. And your journey would not be over when you reached the southern-most point of きゅうしゅう. Approximately 680 kilometres further south-west is an important group of about 60 islands. The largest of these is おきなわ.

The length of Japan means that there is a big difference in climate and lifestyles between ほっかいどう in the far north and おきなわ in the south.

ほっかいどう is known for its cold winters and has many traditions associated with snow and ice.

For example, during February, a snow and ice festival is held in さっぽろ, the main city of ほっかいどう, during which people make large sculptures out of ice like these.

おきなわ, on the other hand, has a much warmer climate. This is reflected in the houses and customs.

Houses on the island of おきなわ

Bullfighting, a sport that people do not usually associate with Japan, is held on おきなわ. Unlike the Spanish variety, in which a man fights a bull, the contest is between two bulls who must try to push each other out of the ring. Because of its distance from Japan and its different customs, people sometimes forget that おきなわ is part of Japan and leave it off the map!

Japan has traditionally been regarded as being part of the Far East.
This came from the days when Britain traded with the Orient.
Is this right when you look where Japan is in relation to your country?
Can you come up with a more accurate term?

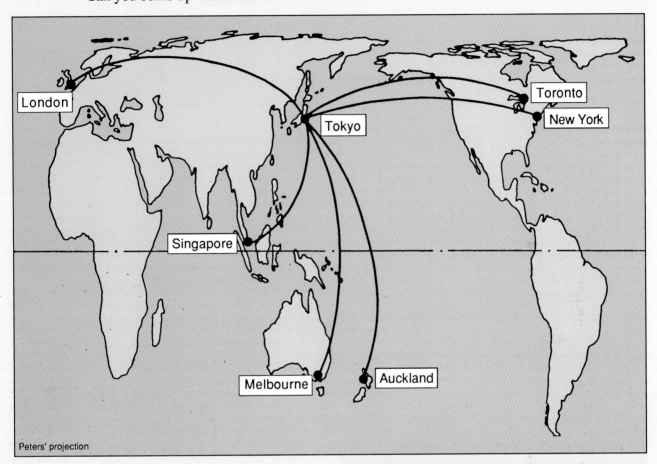

Peters' projection

Use these distances to get a rough idea of how far
Japan is from your part of the world.

Tokyo — Singapore	5,313 km
Tokyo — Melbourne	8,175 km
Tokyo — London	9,555 km
Tokyo — Toronto	10,552 km
Tokyo — New York	10,838 km
Tokyo — Auckland	8,835 km

Islands in Matsushima Bay near Sendai

Mt Fuji

せいかつ

If you have ever been to Japan or seen Japanese visitors, you would have noticed that Japanese people bow a lot. In other countries, people tend to shake hands or kiss when they greet each other, and wave goodbye when they are leaving. In these situations a Japanese person usually bows.

There is a bow for every occasion, from the quick slight bow for friends and family whom you see almost everyday, to the long, low bow used when meeting someone for the first time or when greeting someone who is older than you. But no matter how low or slightly you bow, there is a correct way to do it - you must bend from your waist, keeping the whole top half of your body relatively straight.

こんにちは。

こんにちは。

Bowing has always played a big part in Japanese life. Hundreds of years ago in feudal times, failing to bow, or bowing in the incorrect way was considered a very serious offence. While people do not go to the same extreme today, bowing is still a very important part of everyday life in Japan, and people can get offended if they are not bowed to properly. In addition to bowing to everyone you meet in the course of your day, you will always be greeted with a bow when you go into shops. In the big department stores that Tokyo and other cities in Japan are so famous for, you'll often find a person who bows and greets everyone who enters the shop. Even when you draw money out of the automatic teller machines, you'll be greeted by a little computer-simulated man, who bows in his stilted way and welcomes you to the bank!

Japanese people also bow when they are thanking someone. For some people, it is such an automatic reaction that they even bow when thanking someone on the telephone!

ありがとう
ございます。

One more very important situation in which you need to bow in Japanese, is when you are apologising to someone, like the man on this sign. The sign is to let people know that something is under construction, and apologises for any inconvenience.

御通行中の皆様へ

工事中は何かと、ご迷惑を
おかけ致して居ります
安全には充分気を付けて
作業しておりますので
しばらくの間ご協力を
お願い致します。

Depending on how much you have offended the other person, you may want to bow very low, until the top half of your body is at right angles to the rest of your body. What do you think this man is saying and why?

すみません。

がんばれ！

か よ お ネ モ ル 本 家 花

や ち ぬ キ タ オ 車 日 駅

Japanese writing

All of the Japanese words you have seen so far have been written in Japanese writing, which is certainly very different from how we write in English.

There are actually three types of Japanese writing. They are called *hiragana*, *katakana* and *kanji*. Japanese sentences are usually a mixture of all three of them.

Hiragana （ひらがな）

Almost all of the words appearing in the cartoon story are written in *hiragana*. There are forty-six basic *hiragana* symbols and soon you will learn to read and write all of them. Another example of *hiragana* appears on the cover of this book. Can you guess what it says?

Katakana （カタカナ）

You will have noticed that in the cartoon story some of the characters names are written in what seems like English. What are their names?

If you look closely, you'll see that they are not necessarily spelt in the same way as they are in English. These names are spelt according to the way Japanese people say them. Do you know how to say your name the Japanese way?

Japanese people write foreign names like these in *katakana*. For example, in *katakana* Amanda's name is written アマンダ. In fact, in Japanese all words borrowed from other languages are written in *katakana*. However, as you are just starting to learn Japanese, in this book all of these words will be written in our English letters. Whenever Japanese words or Japanese-style foreign words are written in our letters like this, it is called *roomaji*.

Kanji （漢字）

The numbers *one* to *six* which appear in the cartoon story are written in a different system of writing called *kanji*. Using *kanji* is a more sophisticated way of writing Japanese. *Kanji* can be used instead of *hiragana* to represent a whole word or a part of a word.

Some words that are used a lot are never written in *hiragana*. For example, you almost never write the numbers in *hiragana*, but you can like this,

一・いち　二・に　三・さん　四・よん or し　五・ご　六・ろく

Another example is the word for the Japanese language. It is written にほんご in *hiragana*, but because it is such a common and important word, you are more likely to see it written in *kanji* like this: 日本語.

Some *kanji* came from pictures, for example, the *kanji* for *mountain* and *river* developed like this:

山 mountain

川 river

日本語 *nooto*

一 Greeting people

おはよう。 This is like saying *morning!* You can say it to friends and people you know really well. When you are talking to an adult, or someone you don't know very well, you must say おはよう ございます.

In the cartoon story, you'll notice that the characters greeted each other with おはよう, but when they greeted the teacher, they said おはよう ございます.

Both these greetings are used only in the morning, until about 11.00 a.m.

こんにちは。 This means *hello*, and is used from 11.00 a.m. until around 5 o'clock in the evening. After that, you use こんばんは, which means *good evening*.

二 Saying goodbye

さようなら。 This is the most common way of saying goodbye in Japanese.
じゃ またね is another more casual way of saying goodbye and is like saying *see you later*. It's best to use さようなら with adults.
おやすみ なさい is the expression you use when you're off to bed.

三 えっ!?

えっ!? can be roughly translated as *what's this?!* and you use it when you are shocked and surprised at something that someone has said or done and want some explanation.

四 Addressing people

たなかさん	Mr/Mrs/Miss/Ms Tanaka
はなこさん	(Miss) Hanako
Hose くん	(Mr or Master) Jose
ほんだせんせい	Mrs/Miss/Ms Honda

All of the above words in red are forms of addressing people, or titles. As you can see in the above examples, titles are used in Japanese in many cases where you don't use them in English. In fact, whenever you use someone's name in Japanese, you usually add a title. However, you never use a title after your own name.

The most common one is さん, which can be used with everyone except small children. くん is a common alternative to さん for boys. As you know せんせい means *teacher*, and is generally used with teachers' names instead of さん. However, when you are talking directly to the teacher, just use せんせい.

e.g. せんせい、おはよう ございます。
Good morning Miss/Sir.

五 Apologising

すみません is a quick and easy way to apologise in most circumstances, such as when you're late for class.

You also use this expression when you want to get someone's attention. In this case it means *excuse me*.

おめでとう!

Now you can do all of the following things in Japanese.

· greet people at any time of the day
· ask for someone's name
· say what your name is
· say goodbye
· apologise for something you have said or done
· show that you are surprised
· count to six, and recognise the *kanji* for these numbers

きもの2・おなまえは？

すみません。

ぼくは Hose です。
どうぞ よろしく。

ほん です。
どうぞ。

これは えんぴつ ですか。

はい、えんぴつ です。

これは なん ですか。

ふでばこです。　どうぞ。

ありがとう。　おなまえは?

いいましょう 一

一	はなこさん
二	ゆうこさん
三	としおくん
四	Hose くん
五	みちこさん
六	Amanda さん
七	Popi さん
八	Jiangu くん
九	Mario くん
十	Tonii くん

Talk about the volleyball team using the examples as a guide.

例:

A 一ばんは はなこさん ですか。

B はい、はなこさん です。

例:

A 一ばんは ゆうこさん ですか。

B いいえ、はなこさん です。

例:

A 二ばんは?

B ゆうこさん です。

八ばんは としおくん
ですか。

はい、としおくん です。

いいましょう 二

なんさい ですか

としお 12　　あきお 12　　たろう 13

ゆうこ 12　　ひろこ 13　　かずみ 12

Talk about the each photo using the example as a guide.

例:

A ゆうこさんは なんさい ですか。
B 十二さい です。

Now practise giving your own age.

なんさい ですか。

三さい です。

いいましょう 三

一二三四五六七八九

ほん
pen
けし gomu
ふでばこ
ものさし
えんぴつ
こくばん
まど
doa

Talk about the picture using the examples as a guide.

例:

A 日本語で なん ですか。
B えんぴつ です。

例:

A ほん です。 どうぞ。
B ありがとう。

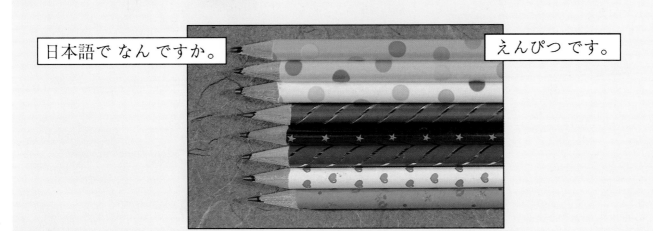

日本語で なん ですか。

えんぴつ です。

きいて いいましょう

一　Listen to the characters speaking in turn. Can you identify who is speaking? Here is an example.

一

例:
Hose くん です。

二

三

四

五

六

二　なん ですか

Listen to the sounds made by these objects. Can you identify the object in each case? Say what it is in Japanese. Here is an example.

一

二

三

例:
ほん です。

四

五

いきいきと はなしましょう

一 おなまえは? What's your name?

From now on in Japanese classes, it's a good idea to use only your classmates' Japanese-style names when talking to them. But first of all, do you remember how to say your own name in Japanese?

The teacher begins by indicating one of you and asking your name. You have to reply with your name in Japanese. Now it's your turn to get the attention and ask the name of someone else in the class. Continue in this way until everyone has had a go. Listen carefully as each name is said, as you may be asked to recall it later.

When the teacher is satisfied that you all know how to say your own names, see if you can remember the names of other people in your class. Someone begins by indicating another person and saying ...さん です or ...くん です. Whoever has been named then continues by indicating another person and saying their name. Continue in this way until everyone has been named. No-one is to be named twice.

二 なんさい ですか How old are you?

You have to pick an under-14 basketball team from members of your class. You'll need six players who are under 14 at the 1st August. Ask how old people are in your class, and stop when you have found six people who are the right age.

三 How well do you know your numbers in Japanese?

Count from one to ten over and over again around the class or in groups, missing out a different number each time. The first time you count to ten, you miss out the number one, the next time two, then three, etc.
If someone makes a mistake, they have to sit down.

See how long you can continue until there is only one person left standing.

Practise counting in Japanese.

六... 七... 八... 九... 十...

がんばれ!

日本語 の はつおん

Learning Japanese is different from learning some other languages, such as French and Italian, because it has a different writing system. In languages which use the roman script, you can often recognise words which are similar in English, and this helps you to remember them. In Japanese, until you can read the script, you can't rely on your eyes to remember words, you have to listen very carefully - you have to rely on your ears. In the beginning the way you learn Japanese is a bit like the way you learned your first language. That is you listen and imitate what you hear.

When you're just starting to speak another language, it's tempting to pronounce words in the same way as you would in English. For example, you probably already know words like *kimono* and *sayonara*. However, if you listen carefully to a Japanese person saying these words, you'll notice that they say them quite differently from the way we say them in English.

It is very important to make an effort to get your pronunciation right. This can be hard at first, because your mouth is used to forming English sounds. And you might feel embarrassed as your mouth forms strange shapes and you hear yourself producing unfamiliar sounds. But it is worth the effort. Think about your reaction when you hear someone speaking English with a heavy accent.

In Japanese, initially the most important sounds to master are the vowels. There are five basic vowel sounds in Japanese. Once you know how to say them properly, the rest is relatively easy. Other sounds are made by adding different consonants to these vowels.

たんご

New words and expressions	
ありがとう __	thank you
いいえ __	no
これ __	this
...さい __	...years old
どうぞ __	here you are
どうぞ よろしく __	pleased to meet you
なんさい ですか __	how old are you?
なん ですか __	what is it?
日本語 (にほんご)で なん ですか __	what is it in Japanese?
はい __	yes
...ばん __	number...
ぼく(は) __	I (men and boys only)
わたし(は) __	I

In the classroom	
えんぴつ __	pencil
けしgomu __	rubber
こくばん __	blackboard
doa __	door
ふでばこ __	pencil-case
pen —	pen
ほん __	book
まど __	window
ものさし __	ruler

More numbers			
七 __	seven	__	なな or しち
八 __	eight	__	はち
九 __	nine	__	きゅう or く
十 __	ten	__	じゅう
十一 __	eleven	__	じゅういち
十二 __	twelve	__	じゅうに
十三 __	thirteen	__	じゅうさん

せいかつ

日本にいきましょう！ Let's go to Japan!

Imagine you are planning a trip to Japan.
Here are some of the things you need to work out
before you leave.

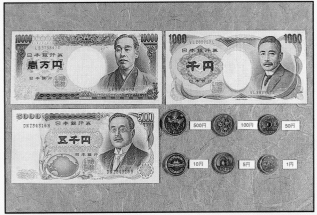

· You would like to be in Japan in spring to see
the cherry blossom. What month would be a good
time to arrive?

· How long will the trip take you? You can work
it out roughly if you know the approximate
distance and the average speed of a modern jet.
You can check the approximate distance from
your part of the world to Tokyo on page 8, and
nowadays a jet can average about 800 kilometres
per hour. Don't forget to allow three or four hours
for stopovers. Check your answer with someone
who has been there.

· Can you really afford to go? Try and find out
how much the trip will cost.

· Which airline will you choose? Why?

· What documents do you need before you leave?
What do you have to do to get them?

· You will need different currency in Japan.
What is Japanese currency called? How will you
change your money? How much is Japanese
money worth in your currency?

· You want to ring your friend in Japan to say
when you are arriving. You want to ring at 8.00
p.m. Japanese time. At what time must you call?

· Which places and cities are you going to visit in
Japan? Why?

· You want to buy a good quality, typically
Japanese product as a present for someone at
home. What will you buy? Where will you get it?

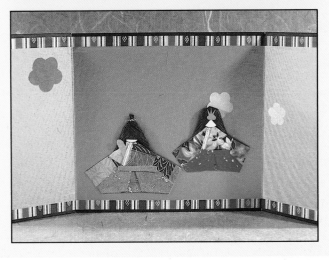

日本語 nooto

一 です

です is a very useful little word in Japanese. It can be used in a number of cases where we need to use different words in English. In this unit we have already seen it has at least three different meanings:

a) *I am*
e.g. （わたしは）はなこ です。
I'm Hanako.
（ぼくは）Hose です。
I'm Jose.

b) *it is, this is*
e.g. ほん です。
It's a book.
ふでばこ です。
It's a pencil-case.

c) *he is, she is, that is*
e.g. はなこさん です。
She's Hanako. / That's Hanako.
Hose くん です。
He's Jose. / That's Jose.

You can see from the examples that is not always necessary to use わたしは or ぼくは. Usually it is clear from the context who you are talking about.

二 Asking questions

Asking questions in Japanese is easy. All you have to do is add か to the end of a sentence, and put a questioning tone into your voice.

e.g. はなこさん です。
That's Hanako.
はなこさん ですか。
Is that Hanako?

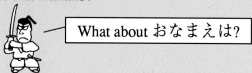

What about おなまえは?

Some questions do not seem to end in か. However, often these are just shortened forms of questions that do end in か.

e.g おなまえは?
What is your name?

This is the shortened form of,
おなまえは なん ですか。

When saying a question like this one, it is important to make it sound like a question. To do this you have to put the question mark into the tone of your voice. You also usually write a question mark. Notice, however, that when a question ends in か you don't need to write a question mark.

三 Talking about yourself

わたしは はなこ です。
ぼくは Hose です。

Both わたし and ぼく mean I, however ぼく is used only by men and boys. Remember never use さん or くん after your own name.

おなまえは？

ぼくは Teo です。

四 Offering something

When you want to give someone something, you say どうぞ. It roughly means *here, take it*.

e.g. ほん です。 どうぞ。
Here's your book.

The person should answer ありがとう, meaning *thank you*.

五 Age

To ask how old someone is in Japanese you say なんさい ですか。
When you are giving your age, you can't just say the number, you must add ...さい です。

e.g. 十三さい です。
I'm thirteen.

うた

Kotsu kotsu

Kotsu kotsu kotsu kotsu
どうぞ、こんにちは。
Kotsu kotsu kotsu kotsu
ありがとう、さようなら。

Kotsu kotsu kotsu kotsu
すみません、おなまえは?
Kotsu kotsu kotsu kotsu
はなこ です。あなたは?

Kotsu kotsu kotsu kotsu
三ばん ですか。
Kotsu kotsu kotsu kotsu
そう です。なん ですか。

Kotsu kotsu kotsu kotsu
きみは なんさい ですか。
Kotsu kotsu kotsu kotsu
三さい です。じゃ またね!

おめでとう!

Now you can do all of the following things in Japanese.

- · introduce yourself to others
- · exchange personal information
  - · ask someone's name
  - · say who you are
  - · ask someone's age
  - · say how old you are
- · offer something to someone and say thank you
- · count to thirteen, and recognise the *kanji* for these numbers

ひらがな 一

The Japanese *hiragana* chart is the equivalent of our alphabet. However, the Japanese 'alphabet' is a bit different from the English one. Each *hiragana* stands for a syllable rather than a single letter.

Syllables can be any one of the vowels, *a, i, u, e, o,* or a combination of one or two consonants plus a vowel.

You have already seen many of them. Now it's time to learn to read and write all of them. Can you recognise any?

	A	I	U	E	O
	あ	い	う	え	お
K	か	き	く	け	こ
G	が	ぎ	ぐ	げ	ご
S	さ	し (shi)	す	せ	そ
Z	ざ	じ (ji)	ず	ぜ	ぞ
T	た	ち (chi)	つ (tsu)	て	と
D	だ	(ぢ) (ji)	(づ) (zu)	で	ど
N	な	に	ぬ	ね	の
H	は	ひ	ふ (fu)	へ	ほ
B	ば	び	ぶ	べ	ぼ
P	ぱ	ぴ	ぷ	ぺ	ぽ
M	ま	み	む	め	も
Y	や		ゆ		よ
R	ら	り	る	れ	ろ
W	わ				を (o)
N	ん (n)				

The ひらがな chart

Look again at the ひらがな chart. Use this chart when you need to check how to read the ひらがな symbols. You can read the symbols in any line by combining the consonant at the beginning of the line with the vowel at the top of each column. For example, か is in the line beginning K under the A column, so you read it as KA.

Unfortunately, there are a few exceptions. Some ひらがな do not exactly follow this rule. In these cases, the *roomaji* reading is shown beside them on the chart. For example, し is read SHI not SI. Find the other ones like this on the chart.

は is another symbol that does not exactly follow the same rule. It can be read in two ways. On the chart it is in the line beginning H under the A column, so you read it as HA. But sometimes it can be read as WA. You'll find out more about this later. You have already seen examples of both readings. Do you recognise these words? In which words is は read HA and in which ones is it read WA?

こんにちは
はなこさん
こんばんは
おはよう

Just as the letters in our alphabet are in a certain order, ひらがな are arranged in a certain order on the chart. You obtain the order by reading the chart from left to right across the page. Telephone books in Japan and the dictionaries that Japanese people use follow this order. In きもの, the word lists in each unit and at the back of the book also follow this order.

がんばれ!

Until you know the ひらがな symbols, they can just look like a lot of squiggles and curves that don't mean anything. However, as you learn to read and write ひらがな, you'll find a whole new world opening up, and soon you'll never look at them in the same way again.

Learning to read and write ひらがな is no small task, so here are some hints on how to do it.

· Set yourself a target of learning say five a day.
· What does each ひらがな remind you of?

See if you can see a picture in each one which will remind you of how to say it. Here's an example.

If you look for this ひらがな on the chart, you'll find that it is in the line beginning Y under the O column. So, you say *yo*. A good way to remember this one is to imagine that it looks like a yacht. Even though it is not spelt in the same way, *yo* is the same sound at the beginning of *yacht*.

See if you can think of similar ideas for other ひらがな.

· After you have done some writing practice in your *Workbook*, write the ひらがな onto small cards. You could then punch a hole in one corner of each, and thread them onto a key ring. Then, whenever you have a spare moment, for example on the bus home from school, take out your stack of cards and test yourself.

か...き...く...

· Get together with a friend and test each other using your cards.

These are just some suggestions. Why not have a discussion in class to see if the others have some good ideas for learning and remembering ひらがな. Remember, the way you learn is very personal: what works for you, may not work for other people, and vice versa.

よみましょう！

きもの

うちわ

いぬ

うさぎ

こいのぼり

すみません！

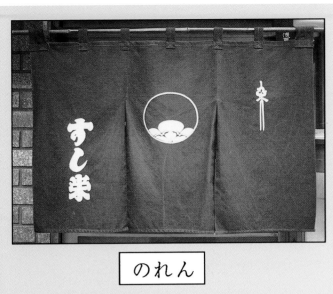

のれん

えき

つき

ほし

おはし

ごはん

うち

おりがみ

しんかんせん／ふじさん

Writing ひらがな

Learning to write ひらがな isn't like anything you have done before. And as with anything new you need to do a lot of practice before you master it.

You'll be doing lots of writing practice in your *Workbook*, but first here are some important points to remember when writing ひらがな.

· Each ひらがな is made up of a number of lines called strokes.

· ひらがな are balanced. They should not look crooked or as if they are about the fall over! The length of the strokes, their angle to one another and the space between them are important in making a ひらがな symbol balanced.

Let's look at an example.

In this symbol the vertical line is longer than the horizontal one. The curved line is drawn at a particular angle to the vertical one and contains a space.

Drawing a small circle is a useful way of showing that a space should be left, but notice that it is not a part of the symbol.

What can you say about the length, angle and space of the strokes in the following symbols?

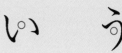

The angle of the page on your desk is also important when writing Japanese. You are more likely to write balanced ひらがな if you place your page squarely in front of you.

· Strokes must be written in a certain order. If you don't follow the correct order, then it is hard to make the symbol look balanced.

Look at the following symbol. What is it? Follow the order of the strokes to see how it is written.

You call the strokes by the numbers, 一, 二, 三, 四, 五 etc. How many strokes are there in the above symbol?

A general rule for drawing the strokes in the correct order is to start from the left-hand side and do the horizontal line first. Vertical lines are drawn from top to bottom.

The way in which strokes are drawn, and in particular, how they end, is also important. For example, the last stroke in な ends abruptly. To achieve this, you take your pen or pencil off the paper as soon as you have finished drawing the stroke.

The first and third strokes of か, on the other hand, have a slight hook on the end. Then some strokes finish with a sweeping motion, for example, つ. You can see that the line gradually fades away. Can you find any others that finish in this way?

Japanese is traditionally written vertically or down the page. Japanese people start writing from the top right-hand corner of the page and write downwards. What effect do you think this has on the way Japanese books open?

However, horizontal writing is becoming increasingly popular in Japan. You can now find many books which are written across the page.

きもの3・Teriiくん、おやおや！

おかあさん、kooto を かして ください。

え!?

おとうさん、おかあさん、いって きます。

あれ!?

いってらっしゃい。

おばあさん、おはよう ございます。いい おてんき ですね。

あっ！ Sukeeto-boodo ですか。

ええ、そう です。Sukeeto-boodo です。

へええ!!

Amandaさん、たって
ください。

どうぞ。

ありがとう。

Teriiくん ですか。

あっ！Teriiくん！

ええ、そうです。

みなさん、じゃまたね。

おやおや！

⊗⊗

一　きいて

二　みて

三　かして

四　あけて

五　しめて

Give the instruction represented by each picture using the example as a guide.

例:

| A きいて! |
| B きいて ください。 |
| or |
| Teepuを きいて ください。 |

みて!

いいましょう 二

一　おかしい

二　かわいい

三　うるさい

四　すごい

五　きたない

六　おおきい

七　ちいさい

Talk about the pictures using the example as a guide.

例：

A かわいい ですね。
B そう ですね。

きいて いいましょう

⊠⊠　一　Listen to the following sounds. Say in Japanese what you think the person was told to do. Here is an example.

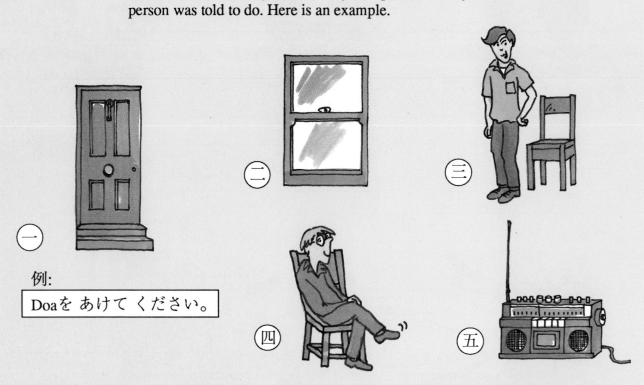

例:

Doaを あけて ください。

二　You'll hear someone comment on these sounds. Say that you agree with them in Japanese. First listen to the example.

例:

そう ですね。

いきいきと はなしましょう

一 Look through your family photograph album or some magazines and find three photographs or pictures that you can describe using two Japanese words. Now, challenge the others in the class to guess which words you thought of.

かわいい です。

ちいさい です。

二 Hose くん...

Jose's main claim to fame is that he has a game named after him called Hose くん. It is similar to *Simon says*!

You take it in turns to be the person who calls out different commands. You only obey the command if the person calling out says ください. For example, if they say

たって ください,

you all stand up. On the other hand, if they just say

たって!

you should ignore it.

きいて ください!

みて ください!

たって ください!

すわって ください!

6th May

3-21, Yukinoshita 1-chome,
Kamakura-shi, Kanagawa-ken,
Japan

Hi everyone,

Sorry I haven't written earlier, but I have been really busy. I have!! Well, I didn't get here until the beginning of April and school started straight away. And once school starts you don't get much time for letter writing. We even have to go on Saturday mornings.

I am in Year 2 at a Junior High School. Classes start at 8.30 every morning, except Mondays when we have assembly in the gym. You should see the assembly. There are about 1,500 students - more, probably - and it's like this huge dark sea of people with black hair and blue uniforms. There's this red-haired boy from California at the school as well and he really stands out. I suppose I do too. The boy's name is Scott.

In winter the boys wear these sort of old-fashioned army officers' jackets with polished buttons and stiff collars. I think the boys should all wear them at school back home! By the way, it's not just our school that has this uniform. The only difference in uniform from school to school is a sort of badge you clip onto it which shows which school you go to. And of course you never wear your outside shoes inside the school. You take them off at the shoe locker and put on gym shoes.

I'm getting used to the uniform. Just as well, I suppose, because the school is pretty strict about it. It's a sort of sailor suit with a long pleated navy blue skirt. Most of the girls are looking forward to getting to Senior High where they can wear a blazer instead of the sailor suit. You know my big sister Giselle, well that's where she goes while we are here. Even in Senior High they seem pretty strict about the length of the skirts. And no perms, no pierced ears! The girls here are really jealous of me and say that they are coming to visit me at home and the first thing they'll do is get a perm. My best friend, Eriko, says that she would get her ears pierced and after school every day she would go to a coffee shop and just sit around because the school doesn't let them do that sort of thing here.

It's really hard to get used to the size of classes here. There are 47 students in mine and it's really hard to get to know all their names. You're not allowed to sit next to your friends. Everyone is in rows facing the front. You don't say much in class. The teacher sort of just gives out the information and it's up to you to try and follow what's going on. You don't have lots of discussions and stuff like we have at home.

They say the best way to get to make friends is in the after-school clubs. You see, that's another reason I haven't been able to write. It's not like you just go home at 3.15 when school finishes. Just about everyone stays at school for some sort of club. All the club leaders have been treating me like a real celebrity, trying to get me to join them. The choir tried first but lost interest after they heard me sing. Then the newspaper club interviewed me. It's funny, they didn't ask me much about back home, they were more interested to know what I liked and didn't like about Japan - especially what Japanese foods I could or couldn't eat.

Of course, the English club tried to get me too. The president or whatever gave me this present which he didn't have to do. I said I would go and speak at their club sometimes. They think I'm fantastic at English but if I don't get 100 in every test they think there's something wrong. Sometimes I have trouble reading the instructions in the tests. We have quite a lot of tests. I went into one of the English classes and spoke to the students. I was really nervous. The teacher was really nice, but he corrected my pronunciation when I said tomato and vase the way we say those words at home. I thought that was a bit of a funny thing to do.

Anyway, I finally decided to join the けんどう club. けんどう is sort of Japanese fencing, but the best part is you get this fantastic armour with your own name written in Japanese on it. I hope I can keep it up when I get back home. It's better than じゅうどう and からて, I think. Actually, I might join another club as well because some of my friends here go to cram school two nights a week and I'm not going to do that. They tell me they have to do it or other kids will get better than them and will get into the better Senior Highs. It's just so competitive here. But it must be a bit boring having to go to school at night as well and

sit in another big class. At least Japanese kids don't get all that much homework. Anyway, I thought I might join the calligraphy club and learn to do that beautiful Japanese writing with a brush.

So you can see I've been really busy. Wait, I nearly forgot about school cleaning duty. Everyone has to clean the school every day. I have to help in the gym and we don't get mops or anything, just a bit of cloth and we have to bend over and run along wiping the floor. And you should see the old-fashioned brooms the outside cleaners get. The kids in the photo cleaning up the streets have volunteered to do extra cleaning! I thought Japan had a machine for every job! Sometimes you have to yell at a couple of the kids to make sure they do their share and don't go off shooting baskets or something. And you should see the gym. It's unbelievable. It's huge and it's got just about every bit of equipment you could imagine. That's where I do けんどう. It's always being used for basketball or table tennis or something. Even in the holidays. So is the pool.

I've got to go now. My host family is taking me to meet some more of their friends. They're really nice, but they keep offering me food and they sort of worry about you if you don't keep eating. And if you do, they just keep bringing you more food. You should see how fat I'm getting. I think I'd better join the jogging club at school.

Please write soon and tell me all your news.

Lots of love,

Simone

たんご

Expressions

あれ!?	look! heavens above!
いい おてんき ですね	it's a nice day today, isn't it?
いってきます	goodbye (used by the person leaving)
いって らっしゃい	goodbye (used by the person remaining)
ええ	yes, yeah
おやおや!	oh dear!
そう ですね	that's right, I agree
へええ!	huh!

New words

おかあさん	mother, Mum
おとうさん	father, Dad
おばあさん	old lady, madam
ください	please
kooto	coat
sukeeto-boodo	skateboard
…ね	expressing agreement (e.g. ...isn't it, etc.)

Adjectives

うるさい	noisy, annoying, loud
おおきい	big
おかしい	funny
かわいい	cute, sweet
きたない	dirty, untidy
すごい	great, fantastic
ちいさい	small

がんばれ!

Looking for similarities and differences in ひらがな

Do you remember when every ひらがな symbol looked the same, a lot of squiggles and curves that did not mean anything?

Now you have made the effort to learn them, you are probably finding that each symbol is gradually taking on its own identity and it is hard to imagine that you ever felt like that. おめでとう!

However, learning ひらがな does not stop just because you have completed the ひらがな unit. To completely master ひらがな you need to continually use it, both in reading and writing.

You may find that you always get some mixed up. Some ひらがな look so much alike that it is easy to get them confused.

For example, い and り are very similar in that they are both made up of two vertical strokes.

The main difference between them is that い has a long left stroke, while り has a long right stroke. If you learn similar symbols together and focus on the difference between them, it makes them easier to remember.

Here are some more pairs and groups of symbols that are easy to confuse.

さ and き
ろ and る
ぬ, ね, め, わ and れ
さ and ち
に and た
い and こ
ち and ら
は and ほ

What makes them similar? How are they different?

日本語 nooto

一   Asking people to do things

a) すわって!   Sit down!
きいて!   Listen!
みて!   Look!

As a student of Japanese, it is important that you understand these and other instructions given to you by your Japanese teacher in class. Study the above examples. Do they have anything in common? If so, what is it?

b) Now, look closely at the following examples.

すわって ください。   Sit down, please.
きいて ください。   Listen, please.
みて ください。   Look, please.

In all of these examples ください means *please*. As in English, you can sometimes leave off ください. For example, if you are getting exasperated that someone is not listening to you, you might say きいて!
However, in some circumstances this can sound rude, so as a general rule it is better to always say ください

c) かして ください。
Lend it to me, please.
Kootoを かして ください。
Lend me the coat, please.
しめて ください。
Close it, please.
Doaを しめて ください。
Close the door, please.

The second sentence in each of these pairs is more specific than the first. You are saying exactly *what* you want to borrow and *what* you want to be closed. These are the objects of the instruction. The *object* is always followed by を.
Here are some more examples.

Teepuを きいて ください。
Listen to the tape, please.
みなさん、こくばんを みて ください。
Look at the blackboard, everyone.

二   Agreeing

When you make a comment that you think the other person will agree with, you add ね to the end of the sentence. It is like saying *isn't it?*

e.g.   かわいい ですね。
It's cute, isn't it?
いい おてんき ですね。
It's a nice day, isn't it?

When you want to show that you agree with something that someone has said, you say そう ですね (that's right, I agree).

三   Asking people how they are

In Japanese it is not as common as it is in English to ask someone, *how are you?* as a way of starting a conversation. It is more usual to make a comment about the weather.

e.g.   いい おてんき ですね。
It's a nice day, isn't it?

おめでとう

Now you can do all of the following things in Japanese.

· understand and give some of the instructions likely to be given in your Japanese classes
· describe things and people
· agree with people when they make comments

おおきい ですね。   そう ですね。

たんじょうび おめでとう！

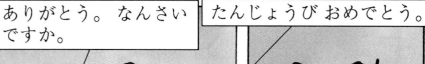

いいましょうー

⊗⊗

たんじょうびは いつ ですか

一がつ (一月)

日	月	火	水	木	金	土
	1	2	3	4	5	6
7	8	9	10	11	12	13
14	15	16	17	18	19	20
21	22	23	24	25	26	27
28	29	30	31			

五がつ (五月)

日	月	火	水	木	金	土
		1	2	3	4	5
6	7	8	9	10	11	12
13	14	15	16	17	18	19
20	21	22	23	24	25	26
27	28	29	30	31		

九がつ (九月)

日	月	火	水	木	金	土
30						1
2	3	4	5	6	7	8
9	10	11	12	13	14	15
16	17	18	19	20	21	22
23	24	25	26	27	28	29

二 がつ (二月)

日	月	火	水	木	金	土
					1	2	3
4	5	6	7	8	9	10
11	12	13	14	15	16	17
18	19	20	21	22	23	24
25	26	27	28			

六がつ (六月)

日	月	火	水	木	金	土
					1	2
3	4	5	6	7	8	9
10	11	12	13	14	15	16
17	18	19	20	21	22	23
24	25	26	27	28	29	30

十がつ (十月)

日	月	火	水	木	金	土
	1	2	3	4	5	6
7	8	9	10	11	12	13
14	15	16	17	18	19	20
22	23	24	25	26	27	28
29	30	31				

三がつ (三月)

日	月	火	水	木	金	土
					1	2
4	5	6	7	8	9	10
11	12	13	14	15	16	17
18	19	20	21	22	23	24
25	26	27	28	29	30	31

七がつ (七月)

日	月	火	水	木	金	土
1	2	3	4	5	6	7
8	9	10	11	12	13	14
15	16	17	18	19	20	21
22	23	24	25	26	27	28
29	30	31				

十一がつ (十一月)

日	月	火	水	木	金	土
				1	2	3	4
5	6	7	8	9	10	11
12	13	14	15	16	17	18
19	20	21	22	23	24	25
26	27	28	29	30		

四がつ (四月)

日	月	火	水	木	金	土
1	2	3	4	5	6	7
8	9	10	11	12	13	14
15	16	17	18	19	20	21
22	23	24	25	26	27	28
29	30					

八がつ (八月)

日	月	火	水	木	金	土
				1	2	3	4
5	6	7	8	9	10	11
12	13	14	15	16	17	18
19	20	21	22	23	24	25
26	27	28	29	30	31	

十二がつ (十二月)

日	月	火	水	木	金	土
31					1	2
3	4	5	6	7	8	9
10	11	12	13	14	15	16
17	18	19	20	21	22	23
24	25	26	27	28	29	30

Talk about when each character's birthday is using the examples as a guide.

例:

A	Hoseくんの たんじょうびは いつ ですか。
B	二がつ です。

例:

A	二がつ です。
B	Hoseくんの たんじょうび です。

きょうは わたしの たんじょうび です。

たんじょうび おめでとう!

いいましょう 二

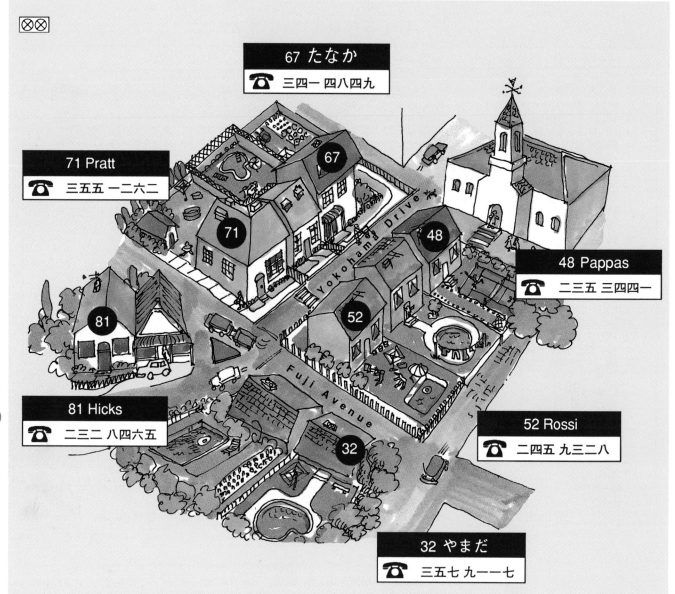

Talk about the picture using the examples as a guide.

例:

A　たなかさんの じゅうしょは?
B　Yokohama Drive の 六十七 ばん です。

例:

A　たなかさんの でんわ ばんごうは なんばん ですか。
B　三四一の四八四九 です。

いいましょう 三

なにどし ですか

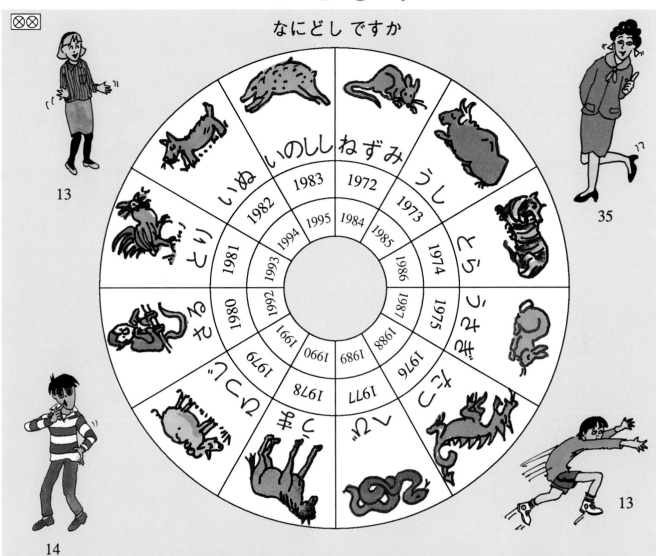

Talk about the じゅうにし using the examples as a guide.

例:

A はなこさんは なんさい ですか。
B 十二さい です。

12   12

例:

A Jiangu くん は なにどし ですか。
B さるどし です。

例:

A Amanda さんは?
B さるどし です。

12

ともだちと

Make up a conversation with a partner. You have to decide who is A and who is B.

A	おはよう。

B	おはよう。

A	おなまえは?

B	みちこ としお たろう	です。	おなまえは?

A	あきお みちこ はなこ	です。	なんさい ですか。

B	十三 十一 十二	さい です。	あきおくん みちこさん はなこさん	は?

A	わたしも わたしは ぼくも ぼくは	十三 十一 十二	さい です。

B	ああ、そう。たんじょうびは いつ ですか。

A	四がつ 八がつ 十一がつ	です。

B	ああ、そう。 なにどし ですか。

A	とらどし うさぎどし いぬどし	です。

いきいきと はなしましょう

一 Divide into small groups of say, five students. You have to find out the age, birthday and じゅうにし animal of each member of the group. Take it in turns to ask each other the questions in Japanese. As each person is interviewed record the details in a grid like the one below.

When each group has finished, combine the information for the whole class and work out what percentage of the class...

· is the same age now
· will be the same age at the end of the year
· is the same animal according to the じゅうにし

例:

なまえ	ねんれい	たんじょうび	なにどし
Catherine	十三さい(13)	八がつ(August)	へび(snake)

二 Two exchange students from Japan are coming to visit your school. You have their photos and some of the information they sent from Japan, including the address and telephone number of where they will be staying here. Your friend has the rest of the information on page 48. You both have to find out the information you are missing by asking each other the right questions in Japanese.

なまえ: やまだ えりこ
ねんれい: 13
じゅうしょ:
でんわ ばんごう: 481 5792

なまえ: すずき あきお
ねんれい:
じゅうしょ: 57 Stokes Avenue
でんわ ばんごう:

なまえ： やまだ えりこ
ねんれい：
じゅうしょ： 39 Kensington
            Road
でんわ ばんごう：

なまえ： すずき あきお
ねんれい： 12
じゅうしょ：
でんわ ばんごう： 586 2194

たんご

New words		
いつ __ when?	paatii __ party	
きょう __ today	bai bai __ bye bye	
じゅうしょ __ address	ひ __ day	
たんじょうび __ birthday	ぼくの __ my (men and boys only)	
でんわ ばんごう __ telephone number	ぼくも __ me too (men and boys only)	
なにどし __ what sign where you born under?	もしもし __ hello (on the telephone)	
	わたしの __ my	
なんばん __ what number?	わたしも __ me too	

Expressions	
ああ、そう __ ah, I see	
ええと __ well then, let's see	
えっ、なに？ __ what?	
さあ __ um..(I don't know)	
じゃ あとで __ see you in a little while!	
じゃあね __ see you!	
たんじょうび おめでとう！ __ happy birthday!	
ほんとう __ really?	
わかりました __ I understand	
わかりません __ I don't understand	

うた

はなこさんの まきばで

はなこさんの まきばで
Ii ai, ii ai, oo
おや ないてるのは いぬ
Ii ai, ii ai, oo
あら wan wan wan, ほら wan wan wan
あっちも、こっちも、どこ でも wan wan
はなこさんの まきばで
Ii ai, ii ai, oo

(In each remaining verse, substitute the following
words for the words in blue.)

Verse 2
うま
hi hi-n, hi hi-n, hi hi-n

Verse 3
とり
chi, chi, chi

Verse 4
うし
mo-, mo-, mo-

Verse 5
ねこ
nyaa-o, nyaa-o, nyaa-o

Verse 6
あひる
gaa, gaa, gaa

Verse 7
かえる
kero, kero, kero

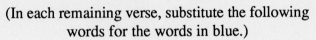

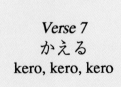

3-21, Yukinoshita 1-chome,
Kamakura-shi, Kanagawa-ken,
Japan

20th May

Hi everyone,

Well, I haven't told you much about the Tanakas yet. They're the people I'm staying with, and they're really nice. They are really polite and they treat me really well, being a visitor. Like I always get served second, after Mr Tanaka, that's if he's home, and I also get second bath.

Well, you see, Japanese houses have these deep baths and you don't get into them until you've washed and rinsed yourself really properly. You do that at a sort of special tiled area near the bath. You sit on a special stool and use a sort of bucket. Mrs Tanaka has been looking at brochures with hand held showers in them so they might be going to change over from the bucket system. The bath is full of this really hot water and you just sit there and relax.

The first time I had a bath I thought I'd do the right thing and when I had finished I let the water out. While all this hot water was going down the plug I could hear the other people in the family saying my name and sounding a bit upset. When I got out no one said anything but a bit later the little girl, Haruko, came up and told me that I had ruined everything because everyone was waiting to use the same water. How embarrassing! Anyway, I'm used to it now and sometimes Haruko comes and jumps in the bath with me and just talks away in this fantastic Japanese.

Little kids are really brilliant in Japan. You should see them speak the language. Haruko is only four and she speaks it so well and she can't understand why I find it so hard. Sometimes when I say things she just giggles. And then she expects me to read her bedtime stories for her and I can only read little bits. She is learning ひらがな herself. Her mum puts new characters on the fridge door every day. It helps me as well. It's a bit like the way our teacher puts things up in the classroom back home.

This is Haruko and some of her friends. She's the one at the end.

Haruko is really cute but she's really bossy. Like when I used to forget to take off my outside shoes at the entrance she would always tell me. And you should see the way she dresses. Her mother always buys this really expensive gear for her. I've never seen her in anything that doesn't have a designer label. Japanese parents seem to spend heaps on their kids. I've already written to tell Mum and Dad about this.

The Tanakas have just moved into this house which is actually built on Mr Tanaka's parents' land. The parents' house is the traditional Japanese style with たたみ mats on the floor and rice

paper sliding screens. Sometimes we eat there and we have to sort of kneel at this very low table. You get used to it.

The Tanaka's new house is two storeys, like most Japanese houses, and it's really nice. It's really modern and Mrs Tanaka keeps it so clean. Even though she's got a part-time job she cleans every bit of the house every day. It's not all that much different from our houses, really - although I've already told you about the bathroom. They seem to have every electrical gadget ever invented. They even have an electric ear cleaner! It really tickles.

I took this photo near our house. My friend Eriko lives in this street.

There is one room in the house which is kept as the traditional Japanese room. It's called the たたみ room. It has たたみ mats on the floor and this is where Mrs Tanaka and her friends do いけばな - that's Japanese for flower arranging- on Wednesday afternoons. That's Mrs Tanaka's job, teaching flower arranging. Mostly she has to go to a school to teach it.

The thing is that the たたみ room is also my bedroom. The Tanakas want me to have a real Japanese experience so I sleep on the traditional Japanese ふとん which is like these layers of mattress on the floor. You have a doona too, of course. And a blanket if you want. It's really comfortable. The thing about the ふとん is that you have to fold it and put it away in the built in cupboard every morning and then you're supposed to clean the room up too. One morning I slept in a bit and didn't sort of get around to doing it. Of course, as soon as I got home Haruko came up and told me that her mother had had to fold up my ふとん and clean my room because I didn't do it. How embarrassing! Anyway, it's all right for her, she sleeps in an ordinary bed and just has to straighten out the doona. I bet she doesn't even do that. Mrs Tanaka does everything.

Well, I'd better go now. First I have to go and walk home with Haruko from piano lessons. She goes twice a week and she's really good. Then we're having a birthday party for Haruko's brother. A couple of friends of his are coming around but I bet they'll probably just stay outside and play 'kyatchibooru' in the street. That's all they ever do, just throw a baseball to each other. They're fanatical about the game. I got him a baseball cap with 'Excellent park champion' written on it. It sounds a bit weird to me but they all had something like that on them.
Hope he likes it.

Bai bai for now now.

Lots of love,

Simone

P.S. That boy Scott I mentioned before is really nice.

日本語 nooto

一　More on numbers

Once you know the numbers up to ten you do not have to learn many more new ones. All of the numbers up to one hundred are a combination of the first ten numbers.

e.g.
十一 _ 11 _ じゅういち
二十 _ 20 _ にじゅう
二十四 _ 24 _ にじゅうよん
四十 _ 40 _ よんじゅう
六十八 _ 68 _ ろくじゅうはち
八十 _ 80 _ はちじゅう
九十一 _ 91 _ きゅうじゅういち
百 _ 100 _ ひゃく

二　What about you?

Amandaさんは なんさい ですか。
How old are you Amanda?

十三さい です。 Jianguくんは?
I'm thirteen. What about you? (literally, what about Jiang?)

In a conversation, instead of repeating the same question that you have just been asked, you can just say the name of the person to whom you are talking, plus は and put a questioning tone in your voice.

三　の

To say *my*, *your*, *his* or *her* in Japanese, you add の to わたし or the person's name.

e.g.　きょうは わたしの たんじょうび です。
Today is my birthday.

はなこさんの いぬ ですか。
Is that Hanako's dog? / Is that your dog, Hanako?

の is also used between words that are connected or belong to one another. In these cases, it is useful to think of の as meaning *of*.

e.g.　Paatii のひ。
The day of the party.

High Streetの なんばん ですか。
What number High Street? (the number of High Street)

Another use of の is in telephone numbers. When you tell someone your telephone number, you usually break it up with a の after the first three numbers.

e.g.　四一八の六七一三　418 6713

四　Can you repeat that please?

If you do not hear what someone says and want them to repeat it, you can simply say, えっ、なに? However, you need to be careful about when you use this expression. It is all right to use it with friends your own age, but it can sound very rude it you use it with someone who is older than you. In this case, you should say, えっ、なんですか。

五　Months

There are no special words for the months in Japanese. They are called by their number plus がつ（月）meaning *month*.

e.g.
January	一がつ	
April	四がつ	（しがつ）
June	六がつ	
July	七がつ	（しちがつ）
September	九がつ	（くがつ）

Notice that 四がつ, 七がつ and 九がつ must be pronounced as shown in the brackets.

六　More on age

Now that you know the numbers up to 100, you can say the age of most people in Japanese: just add the number to さい.

A full list of the numbers plus さい is given in the appendix on page 106.

Notice that the numbers 1, 8 and 10 are pronounced slightly differently when they are combined with さい. However, there is no difference in the way they are written in *kanji*. This pattern is repeated when you want to say 11, 18, 21, 28, 30 etc years old.

e.g. 十一さい is pronounced じゅういっさい

The word for 20 years old does not follow the same pattern. It is はたち. The reason for this is that 20 is an important age in Japan. It is the age when young people become eligible to vote in government elections.

がんばれ!

Looking for 'constants'

Some long sentences can look and sound like one continuous jumble of symbols and sounds.

e.g. はなこさんの でんわ ばんごうは
なんばん ですか。

However, if you can pick out the elements that come up all the time, then long sentences like this one become more manageable.

So what are the elements that come up all of the time? To find out, let's look at some examples of different questions you have seen in this unit.

e.g. Hoseくんは どこ ですか。
たんじょうびは いつ ですか。
ゆうこさんは なんさい ですか。

All of these questions look quite different, but if you look closely you will see that they do have some things which are the same.

In all of them you start off with what or whom you are asking about and add は.
Then you put the question word, for example, どこ, and you finish off with ですか.
は, the 'question word' and ですか are the 'constants' in these questions.

Not only does picking out the 'constants' make long and unfamiliar sentences manageable, it also helps you make up you own. You use the 'constants' as your base, and build around them.

e.g. えんぴつは どこ ですか。
Where's the pencil?
Paatiiは いつ ですか。
When's the party?

Try and make up some more questions like these by using other words instead of えんぴつ and *paatii*, and どこ and いつ.

なにどし ですか。

とりどし です。

わたしも!

おめでとう!

Now you can do all the following things in Japanese.

· give more personal information
  · where you live
  · your telephone number
  · your 'year' sign according to the animal zodiac
  · when your birthday is (the month)
· find out all the above things about other people
· say that you do or don't understand what someone says
· ask someone to repeat something they have said
· count to 100, and read the *kanji* for these numbers

じゅうしょは?

銀座
1丁目
GINZA ST.

You studied all of the basic symbols on the ひらがな chart , in the first ひらがな unit. In this unit you are going to learn about combining some of these symbols to make new sounds.

Little や, ゆ, よ

This chart shows what happens when you combine the sound in the left-hand column with the sounds across the top. When you say them together quickly, you get one sound.

	や	ゆ	よ
き	きゃ	きゅ	きょ
ぎ	ぎゃ	ぎゅ	ぎょ
し	しゃ	しゅ	しょ
じ	じゃ	じゅ	じょ
ち	ちゃ	ちゅ	ちょ
に	にゃ	にゅ	にょ
ひ	ひゃ	ひゅ	ひょ
び	びゃ	びゅ	びょ
ぴ	ぴゃ	ぴゅ	ぴょ
み	みゃ	みゅ	みょ
り	りゃ	りゅ	りょ

Making double vowel sounds

If you say Japanese words slowly out loud you can hear that they are made up of a number of 'beats' - one for each syllable. To pronounce Japanese correctly each 'beat' must be the same length. Try tapping out these words with your finger and count how many 'beats' each one has. Remember that each ひらがな represents one syllable.

こんにちは
せんせい
きたない

You need to be particularly careful about doing this when you come to saying words which have double vowel sounds. It is easy for us to gloss over these as we don't pronounce double vowel sounds in English.

However, in Japanese you have to make a special effort to pronounce the extra vowel sound as a separate 'beat'. If you don't, apart from the fact that it is bad pronunciation, you could be saying something completely different to what you want to say. Look at the following pairs of words.

おばさん　　　　おばあさん
(aunt)　　　　(grandmother, old lady)
とり　　　　とおり
(bird)　　　　(street)

Now practise saying these words out loud.

おはよう
さようなら
おとうさん
かようび

All of these words have a double お sound. When you say these words, you pronounce the う as an お. Most words containing double お sounds are written like this, however not all.

Here are two words that you have seen so far that double the お sound with another お.

おおきい
おおさか

Little つ

a) Do you recognise this symbol - つ?
You have seen it in these words, いつ (when), ひつじ (sheep) and がつ (month).
You have also seen a smaller version of it in words like these,

たって
すわって
いって

When it occurs in a smaller version like this it is not pronounced as つ, it doubles the sound of the consonant that follows.

b) あっ！
　　えっ!?

This is like having two exclamation marks. Both these words or sounds show surprise, and the little つ makes the あ and え sounds shorter and more abrupt.

Writing

In ひらがな一 we talked about the importance of balance and space when writing individual ひらがな symbols. When you come to writing words, then the size of the symbols and the space between them is also important.

Except for the little つ, や, ゆ and よ, all of the symbols should be roughly the same size and evenly spaced. When you are just starting to learn to write it is easier to achieve this by writing in squares like you do in your *Workbook*. No matter the size, each symbol takes up one square.

あ	り	が	と	う		
き	い	て				
お	お	き	い			

Little つ, や, ゆ and よ

Notice how these smaller symbols are written in the examples below. Like the normal sized symbols, they are each entitled to a whole square. When you are writing horizontally, they go in the lower left-hand corner of the square. If you are writing vertically, then you write them in the upper right-hand corner of the square.

き	ょ	う				
じ	ゃ					
じ	ゅ	う	し	ょ		
い	っ	て	ら	っ	し	ゃ	い
た	ん	じ	ょ	う	び		

き	じ	じ	い	た
ょ	ゃ	ゅ	っ	ん
う		う	て	じ
		し	ら	ょ
		ょ	っ	う
			し	び
			ゃ	
			い	

Punctuation

You will have noticed in the cartoon stories that the full stop and commas in Japanese are different from ours. The full stop is called まる and is written as a tiny circle like this, 。 and the comma is known as てん and looks like this, 、

The まる and the てん also take up a whole square.

あ	あ	、	わ	か	り	ま	し	た	。
な	ん	さ	い	で	す	か	。		

Notice that you do not need to use question marks in Japanese. The か is like a question mark.
When a question does not end in か, then you can put a question mark.

e.g. おなまえは? or おなまえは。

ちょうちん

こうえん

あかちゃん

わたし

おにいさん　　おねえさん

きょうだい

がっこう

ざっし

さわやかに旅を行く……

きっぷ

とおり

きって

じゅう(十)

ひこうき

にんぎょう

きもの5 ・ ああ、おいしい！

Hoseくん、じょうず! じょうず!

いいえ...

たんじょうび おめでとう!

おすしは おいしい ですね。

Hoseくん、keeki です。
どうぞ。

ありがとう。

Hoseくんを みて!
おかしい ですね。

むずかしい ですね。

えっ!?

ああ、おいしい!
これは やさしい
ですね。

ごちそうさま。

いいましょう 一

おちゃ

おすし

aisukuriimu

てんぷら

orenji juusu

おかし

hotto doggu

supagetti

karee raisu

piza

hanbaagaa

miruku

やきそば

keeki

koora

koohii

Talk about the pictures and the photographs using these examples as a guide.

例:

A	Hotto dogguは すき ですか。
B	ええ、すき です。
	or
	ええ、だいすき です。
	or
	いいえ、あんまり...

例:

A	Keekiは おいしい ですね。
B	ええ、そう ですね。
	or
	いいえ、まずい です。

やきそばは すき ですか。

はい、だいすき です。

いいましょう 二

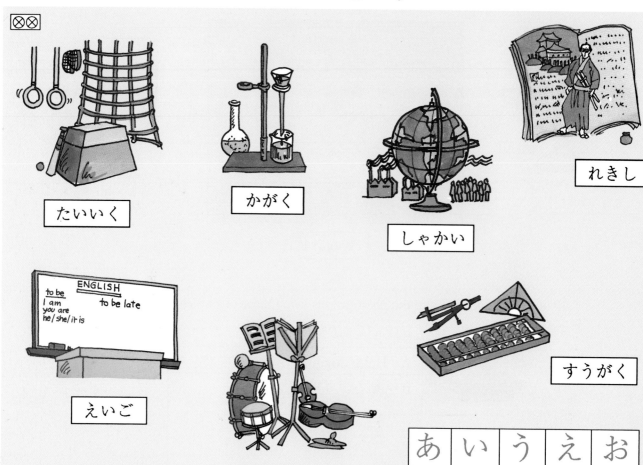

たいいく

かがく

しゃかい

れきし

えいご

おんがく

すうがく

あ　い　う　え　お

日本語

Talk about your school subjects using the examples as a guide.

例:

| A　おんがくは すき ですか。 |
| B　ええ、すき です。 |
| 　　or |
| 　　いいえ、あんまり... |

例:

| A　日本語は やさしい ですね。 |
| B　ええ、そう ですね。 |
| 　　or |
| 　　いいえ、むずかしい です。 |

あ　い　う　え　お

ともだちと

Make up a conversation with a partner. You have to decide who is A and who is B.

Kotsu kotsu

A	ああ、	けいいちくん。 さきこさん。 としおくん。 さちえさん。	どうぞ あがって ください。

B	たんじょうび おめでとう！ Purezentoです。どうぞ。

A	ありがとう。なん ですか。	あっ、	ふでばこ sukeeto boodo おかし ほん	ですね。ありがとう。

B	いいえ。

A	おすし Karee raisu てんぷら おちゃ	は	すき ですか。

B	いいえ、あんまり...

A	じゃ、	keeki aisukuriimu supagetti miruku	は？

B	はい、だいすき です。

A	Keeki Aisukuriimu Supagetti Miruku	です。どうぞ。

B	ありがとう。	Keeki Aisukuriimu Supagetti Miruku	は	おいしい ですね。

いきいきと はなしましょう

一 You're having a birthday party this weekend and your mother said that you can have three different types of food and two drinks. You have to decide which ones you will have.

Choose five foods and three drinks that you think your friends might like to have. Then ask three of your friends in Japanese whether or not they like each one. Record their preferences on a table like the one below.

例:

たべもの/のみもの	ただしくん	Tinaさん	まちこさん	total
hotto doggu	はい	いいえ	はい	2
aisukuriimu	はい	はい	はい	3
piza	はい	いいえ	いいえ	1
supagetti	はい	はい	はい	3
おすし	はい	はい	はい	3
おちゃ	いいえ	はい	いいえ	1
miruku	いいえ	はい	はい	2
koora	はい	いいえ	はい	2

After you have tallied the results, decide the three foods and two drinks you will have at your party.

二 Conduct a survey among members of your class to find out which school subjects are most popular.

First of all, you need to decide on which subjects you are going to include in your survey, and draw up a survey sheet like this one.

例:

	1	2	3	4	5	6	7	8	9	10	total
えいご											
かがく											

Then take a sample of ten students in your class and ask them whether or not they like each subject.

e.g. えいごは すき ですか。

Score their responses like this:

ええ、だいすき です　—　10 points
ええ、すき です　—　7 points
いいえ、あんまり...　—　3 points

Record the scores of each student under one column.

Now add up the number of points for each subject. Which subjects are most popular according to members of your class?

たんご

New words and expressions	
ああ、おいしい！	yum!
どうぞ あがって ください	come in!
おすし	sushi
おそく なって すみません	I'm sorry, I'm late
いただきます	expression used before eating a meal
がんばれ！	come on!
ごちそうさま (でした)	expression used after a meal
...すき ですか	do you like...?
じょうず	good (at something)
でも	but
purezento	present

かもく

えいご	English
おんがく	Music
かがく	Science
しゃかい	Social Studies
すうがく	Maths
たいいく	Phys. Ed.
日本語	Japanese
れきし	History

More adjectives

おいしい	delicious
むずかしい	difficult
まずい	(tastes) awful
やさしい	easy

がんばれ！

Words borrowed from other languages (がいらいご)

Nowadays, with high-speed travel and rapid communication, we know so much more about other cultures. More than ever before, we can welcome some aspects of another culture to extend and enrich our own. As we adopt parts of another culture, we also often borrow some of the language that goes with it.

The most common example of a culture's influence over another is through its food. In English we have borrowed lots of words from French and Italian for food that we have adopted as a part our cuisine. For example, *pizza, quiche spaghetti* and *croissant.* All of these foods are so much a part of our culture now that it is sometimes possible to forget that these words originally came from Italian and French. However, while we use the same word we often don't pronounce it in the same way as Italian and French people do. We say them more like English words.

It is the same in Japanese. They have borrowed many words for the Western-style foods that are now so much a part of their way of life. You have seen many of them in this unit.

e.g. *aisukuriimu, orenji juusu, hotto doggu*

If you say these words out loud, you immediately recognise them as being very similar to English words. The Japanese have borrowed the English word and adapted it to their way of pronunciation. You know from learning ひらがな that all Japanese words are made up of syllables. When a Japanese person comes to say an English word they convert it into Japanese syllables. This is why most of the foreign words converted into Japanese style seem to be stretched out. In this book these words are written in *roomaji*. However, remember that a Japanese person would normally write all of these words in *katakana*.

In English we also use the Japanese words for the Japanese foods we eat. If you have ever been to a Japanese restaurant, you may have tried *tempura* or *sukiyaki*, and you all know what *sushi* (おすし) is now. Has anyone seen a type of apple-like pear in the supermarket lately called a *nashi*? *Nashi* is the Japanese word for *pear*. In Japanese of course, it is written as なし.

せいかつ

おりがみ

One aspect of Japanese culture which has spread all over the world is おりがみ.
おりがみ has become an international hobby. You can find おりがみ clubs all over the world, and books on how to make おりがみ in many languages. Just as the Japanese have borrowed words like *aisukuriimu* and *supagetti* from other languages, the Japanese word おりがみ is used everywhere.

The word おりがみ is made up of two words - おり meaning *fold* and the word for *paper*, かみ/がみ. As its name suggests, おりがみ is the art of folding a single sheet of paper into various shapes.

All Japanese children learn おりがみ in kindergarten and at primary school. However, おりがみ isn't just for children - adults do it too - and everyone enjoys spending many hours trying to create new shapes. In Tokyo there is even an International Research Centre for おりがみ!

The most well-known shape is the つる (crane). The つる is a symbol of good luck. In Japan when someone is sick, often people give them 1,000 folded cranes. These 1,000 cranes are called せんばづる.

Every year on Peace Day (August 6) Japanese children and children from all over the world send せんばづる to Hiroshima to remember the destruction it suffered during World War II. The colourful cranes are draped over many of the statues in the Peace Memorial Park as an expression of hope for a peaceful world.

きもの五　●　六十六

Below are the instructions for making the つる.
Why don't you make せんばづる and send them
to Hiroshima as your gesture to world peace?

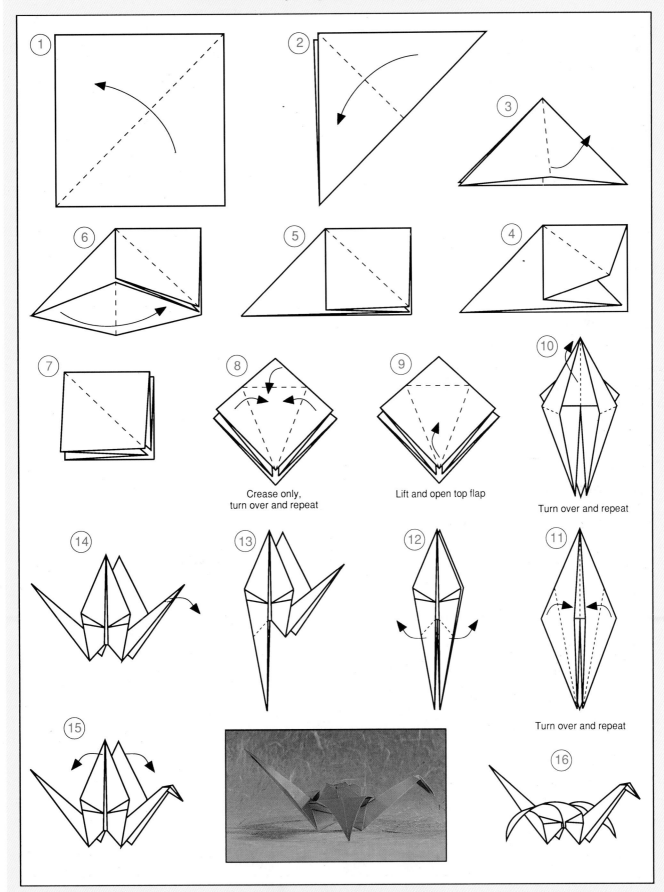

①

②

③

⑥

⑤

④

⑦

⑧ Crease only, turn over and repeat

⑨ Lift and open top flap

⑩ Turn over and repeat

⑭

⑬

⑫

⑪ Turn over and repeat

⑮

⑯

日本語 nooto

一　Making it clear what or whom you are talking about

In Japanese you do not have to specify what or whom you are talking about if it is clear from the context.

e.g. 十二さい です。
おいしい です。

If you look at these examples in isolation, you do not know *who* is 12 and *what* is delicious. However, if someone said them in the middle of a conversation, you would know from what went on before. They would be in context.

If you need to say *what* or *whom* you are talking about, then you say it and add は. So, the above examples could become,

はなこさんは 十二さい です。
Hanako is 12 years old.

おすしは おいしい です。
Sushi is delicious.

This は is pronounced as WA not HA.

二　いいえ

You have seen that いいえ means *no.* It can also mean *that's all right, don't mention it* etc, for example, if someone apologises for being late, thanks you for something, or gives you a compliment.

三　Saying what you like

To ask someone if he or she likes something in Japanese, you say ...はすき ですか。

e.g. おかしは すき ですか。
Do you like sweets?

If someone asks you this question, you can answer,

ええ、すき です。
Yes, I like it.

ええ、だいすき です。
Yes, I love it.

いいえ、あんまり...
No, I don't really...

If you want to say *who* likes or dislikes something, then the は in the question changes to が.

e.g. わたしは おかしが だいすき です。
I really love sweets.

かずこさんは aisukuriimuが すき ですか。
Does Kazuko like ice cream?

わたしは koohii が だいすき です。
I really like coffee.

You will notice in the examples that は follows the person instead.

おめでとう!

Now you can do all of the following things in Japanese.

· talk about what you like and do not like
· talk about food and drink
· discuss your school subjects

げつようびの 四じ です。

Amanda さん! どう
したん ですか。

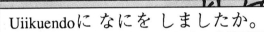

Uiikuendoに なにを しましたか。

ええと、どようびに
terebi を みました。

それは あぶなく ない ですよ。

そう ですね。でも...

そう? それから...?

それから、geemuを しました。

それは あぶなくない ですよ。

そう ですね。
でも、...

あa、わかりました。それから...?

それから、かいものを
しました。

そう ですね。でも、...

それは あぶなく
ない ですよ。

ああ、そう。それから、
なにを しましたか。

それから、hanbaagaaを たべました。
Kooraを のみました。

Amandaさん、どう したん
ですか。

どようびに terebiを みました。
それから、 geemuを しました。

それから、かいものを しました。
Hanbaagaaを たべました。Kooraを
のみました。

それは あぶなく ない ですよ。

これは あぶない ですよ。

いいましょう 一

Uiikuendoに なにを しましたか

一 まんが	四 えいが

二 おんがく	五 koora

三 かいもの	六 hanbaagaa

Talk about the photos using the examples as a guide.

例:

A Uiikuendoに なにを しましたか。
B まんがを よみました。

例:

A おんがくを ききましたか。
B ええ、おんがくを ききました。
or
　いいえ、かいものを しました。

きもの 六 ● 七十二

いいましょう 二

⊗⊗

（一）

（四）

（二）

（五）

（三）
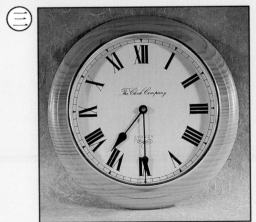

（六）

きもの 六 ● 七十三

Give the time shown on each clock using the example as a guide.

例：

A	いま なんじ ですか。
B	一じ です。
	or
	七じ はん です。

いいましょう 三

じかんひょう

じかん ようび	1	2	3	4	5	6
月	えいご	かがく		しゃかい	おんがく	日本語
火			たいいく	たいいく	えいご	すうがく
水	すうがく	れきし		日本語	かがく	
木	れきし	しゃかい	かがく		えいご	すうがく
金	たいいく	日本語	すうがく			えいご
土	すうがく	しゃかい	しゃかい	日本語		

Talk about the timetable using these examples as a guide.

例:

> A すうがくは いつ ですか。
> B すいようび です。

例:

> A れきしの しゅくだいを しましたか。
> B ええ、しました。
>   or
>   いいえ。でも、日本語の しゅくだいを しました。

Days of the week		
月よう日 __	Monday _____	げつようび
火よう日 __	Tuesday _____	かようび
水よう日 __	Wednesday __	すいようび
木よう日 __	Thursday ___	もくようび
金よう日 __	Friday _____	きんようび
土よう日 __	Saturday ___	どようび
日よう日 __	Sunday _____	にちようび

ともだちと

Make up a conversation with a partner. You have to decide who is A and who is B.

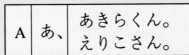

わたしは A です。

ぼくは B です。

A	あ、	あきらくん。 えりこさん。

B	ああ、	ただしくん。 はなこさん。	おはよう。

A	おはよう。	Uiikuendo どようび きんようび にちようび	に	なにを しましたか。

B	Tenisu おんがく えいが からて	を	みました。 しました。 ききました。

A	いいですね。	あきらくん えりこさん	は	すうがく えいご しゃかい	の	しゅくだいを しましたか。

B	ええ、しました。	ただしくん はなこさん	は?

A	わたし ぼく	も	しました。	すうがく えいご しゃかい	は	やさしい ですね。

B	いいえ、むずかしいです。でも、	かがく 日本語 れきし	は	やさしい です。

A	ええ、そうですね。

いきいきと はなしましょう

— How well do you know your friends? If you know someone well, generally you have a good idea of what activities they do on each day of the week.

Make up seven questions for a friend of yours about what they did each day last week and try and predict whether they will answer ええ or いいえ to each of them. Try to think of a different activity for each day of the week.

Write the questions down with your prediction next to each one. Now ask your friend each question. Your friend will do the same for you. At the end you'll see how well you know each other.

Here are some examples of questions you could ask,

にちようびに tenisuを しましたか。
げつようびに すうがくの しゅくだいを しましたか。

To the first question your friend might answer,

ええ、tenisuを しました。 or いいえ、terebiを みました。

がんばれ!

わかりましたか

Here are some important points to remember when you are trying to understand what someone is saying to you in another language.

・Don't be put off if you don't understand every word they say. Focus on what you do understand and use it as a clue to help fill in the gaps.

・Use the context to try to get the overall meaning of what they are saying. You don't need to understand every word, you can usually understand from what is happening around you.

・Listen for the particular information that you need and don't let yourself be distracted by all the other words being spoken around it. For example, if you're listening for page numbers, concentrate all of your attention on listening for the numbers.

・Don't be embarrassed about asking people to repeat things. After all this is a normal part of everyday conversation.

You have probably worked it out for yourself by now - intelligent guessing is one of the most important skills for a foreign language student to develop. The other thing is to act confidently, even if you don't feel it. This is what the people who seem to understand everything are doing.

However, if you really do not understand what someone is saying then you need to know how to stop the conversation and clear up a few points. Here are some useful expressions to know.

すみませんが、よく わかりません...
Excuse me, but I don't understand...

ゆっくり いって ください。
Could you speak slowly, please.

...って、えいごで なん ですか。
What does ... mean in English?

たんご

supootsu

けんどう

tenisu

やきゅう

baree booru

からて

sakkaa

New words and expressions

あぶない	—	dangerous
いま	—	now
uiikuendo（に）	—	(at the) weekend
かいもの	—	shopping
geemu	—	game
それ（は）	—	that
それから	—	then, after that
それは あぶなく ない です	—	that's not dangerous
じかんひょう	—	timetable
しゅくだい	—	homework
terebi	—	television
どう したん ですか	—	what happened?
なに	—	what
まんが	—	comic

Past activities

（を）ききました	—	listened (to)
（を）しました	—	did, played
（を）たべました	—	ate
（を）のみました	—	drank
（を）みました	—	watched
（を）よみました	—	read

せいかつ

3-21, Yukinoshita 1-chome
Kamakura-shi, Kanagawa-ken,
Japan

6th June

Hi everyone,

Well, I'm not boasting or anything but I just thought you'd like to know I got selected as a cheer leader for the school baseball team. I'm really pleased because it was so hard learning all the chants we have to do. We have already played two games and we won them both. They take it pretty seriously.

But the main reason I wanted to write was to tell you about the day we went into Tokyo to get Haruko's new desk. Well, actually, it all started not long after I got here. Haruko's brother, Toshio, had just started primary school and his teacher came around to the Tanaka's to meet the family and to sort of get to know a bit about Toshio's home life. Well, the Tanaka's were really proud because Toshio's new room was really well set up with everything you could possibly want - especially his desk. You should see it! It's huge! And it's got a built-in light, push button controls, built-in calculator, electric pencil sharpeners, everything! It must have cost an absolute fortune.

Well, anyway, one Sunday morning Haruko's grandmother and grandfather were in for breakfast and Haruko started saying that she would soon be starting school and why couldn't she have a desk like Toshio's? The amazing thing was that Grandma Tanaka said yes! Japanese parents and grandparents have this really excellent attitude to kids. So we organised to go into Tokyo that day to this big department store and order a desk for Haruko.

I decided to wear my best outfit because I knew the Tanakas would dress up. Sure enough, they were all in their designer clothes - especially Haruko. She had this expensive looking denim jacket with 'London House Away' written on it. I asked Grandma Tanaka why she wasn't wearing a きもの and she just laughed and said she was too young for that, and anyway she would have trouble keeping up with us because you can only take little steps in them. When I showed her some

young Japanese women in きもの outside the station she said they were probably on the way to a wedding or something special like that.

It wasn't so crowded on the train, being a Sunday. You could even see the floor of the carriage. Japanese trains and buses are absolute luxury. Everything is so clean and new looking. They really look after them. And anyway they don't have all the vandalism and graffiti we have at home. For example, they have these hanging paper advertisements in the carriages and nobody touches them. It's unbelievable. They were changing them that Sunday and the man gave me one as a souvenir.

I was looking forward to seeing central Tokyo. We were going into the Ginza (ぎんざ) which is the most famous street and shopping centre in the city. Mr Tanaka was telling me that in the ぎんざ district the land is the most expensive in the world. That's why they make such good use of the rooftops for things like tennis courts and that.

So we all started to head for the school supplies part of the store. When we got to the escalator there were these escalator girls in beautiful uniforms bowing to everyone who came along, saying things like 'Welcome' and 'Please be careful.' Everyone just seemed to ignore them which I thought was pretty mean, so I stopped and bowed back. They just smiled. I think I held up traffic on the escalator for a while.

It was late afternoon when we eventually got out of that store. It was good because they turn the central area of Tokyo into a 'pedestrian's paradise' on Sundays which is the main shopping day in Japan. This means that traffic isn't allowed in. We strolled around just looking at all the shops. Mr Tanaka stopped outside every sports store looking at golf clubs. He's just fanatical about golf. He goes to the golf driving range near home most Sundays. He said he is hoping to have a game on a real golf course soon but it is really expensive.

After a while we were all getting hungry so we started to look around for a restaurant. The Japanese have a great system for choosing which restaurant to go to. All the food is displayed in the window, except it's not real food, it's plastic. But it looks so real! Mr Tanaka said that there are special plastic food factories. I've put in a photo of one of the windows.

Anyway, I had a 'hanbaagaa' and a 'miruku seeki' (got to have a fix of junk food every so often) and Haruko and Toshio had 'piza' and 'koora'. Haruko didn't eat all of her pizza. It was pretty good, but tasted a bit different from the ones at home. Mr and Mrs Tanaka had 'karee-raisu'. I've never seen Mr Tanaka have a meal without rice. Not even breakfast.

By the time we had finished our meal it was getting dark and all the lights in the ぎんざ were coming on. You should see all the かんじ neon signs when they're all lit up. It's just fantastic. I wish I could read them, though. It gets a bit frustrating at times. But they look just great!

Well, that was our day in Tokyo. I have to go now, my favourite T.V. show is coming on. It's a sort of crazy game show where the contestants have to do all these crazy, dangerous things. I just sit there saying それは あぶない です。 but the Tanakas just laugh. They must be used to it. They love the show too.

Anyway, must go. How about someone writing back?

Lots of love,

Simone

P.S. Haruko's desk arrived the other day. You should see it.

日本語　*nooto*

一　Saying what you did

なにを しましたか。
What did you do?

Terebiを みました。
I watched television.

みちこさんは hanbaagaaを たべました。
Michiko ate a hamburger.

ほんを よみました。
I read a book.

In all of these examples, you are saying *what* you or someone else did. All of the verbs at the end of the sentence end in ...ました. This part of the verb indicates that something has happened.

Notice that *terebi*, *hanbaagaa* and ほん are all followed by を. When you want to say what you did, watched, ate or read etc. you must add を.

二　Saying when something happened

When you are talking about what you did on a particular day of the week, you always say に after the day. In this case it is the same as saying, *on...*

e.g. かようびに けんどうを しました。
　　I did kendo on Tuesday.

The same rule applies to most other 'time' words, like *uiikuendo*.

e.g. Uiikuendoに tenisuを しました。
　　I played tennis at the weekend.

Notice the word order in these sentences. First you say *when* + に, then you say *what* happened.

三　Asking and telling the time

If you want to know the time, you simply ask, いま なんじ ですか。

Here are some answers the other person might give,

一じ です。　　It's one o'clock.
四じ です。　　It's four o'clock.
七じ はん です。　It's half past seven.

じ is another example of a suffix in Japanese used with numbers, and means *o'clock*.
You can say any hour of the day by saying the number plus じ.
Note: 四じ is pronounced よじ
　　　七じ is pronounced しちじ
　　　九じ is pronounced くじ

四　...よ

それは あぶなく ない ですよ。
That's not dangerous!

To emphasise what you think about something you can add よ to the end of the sentence. It is a bit like adding an exclamation mark in English, although you do not stress the よ when you say it.

おめでとう!

Now you can do all of the following things in Japanese.

· tell someone what you did at the weekend
· ask someone what they did
· ask what time it is
· tell someone what time it is (on the hour and half-hour)
· talk about your school timetable

きもの 7・たのしかった ですよ

せんしゅうの どようびに こうえんに いきました。あつかった です。

あつい ですね。

ええ、とても あつい ですね。

あのね、せんしゅう puuruを かいましたよ。

へええ？そう？すごい。

おおきい ですか。

ええ、とても おおきい です。
ごご ぼくの うちに きてね!

ありがとう。
じゃ あとで。

ごご Terii くんの うちに いきました。

pin pon

ああ、みんな...
ちち です。

Uirusonさん、
こんにちは。

みなさん、こんにちは。
どうぞ あがって ください。

にわに いきました。

それ?! あたらしい puuru?!

えっ!

ええ、そう ですよ。どうぞ はいって!

ちいさいですね。

ほんとう?

みんな、まって...

これは わたしの puuru ですよ。
おおきい puuruに いって ください。

おおきい puuru?

Teriiくん、また!

あぶない ですよ。
やめて!

すいえいを しました。それから、
aisukuriimu を たべました。Koora を
のみました。たのしかった です。

いいましょうー

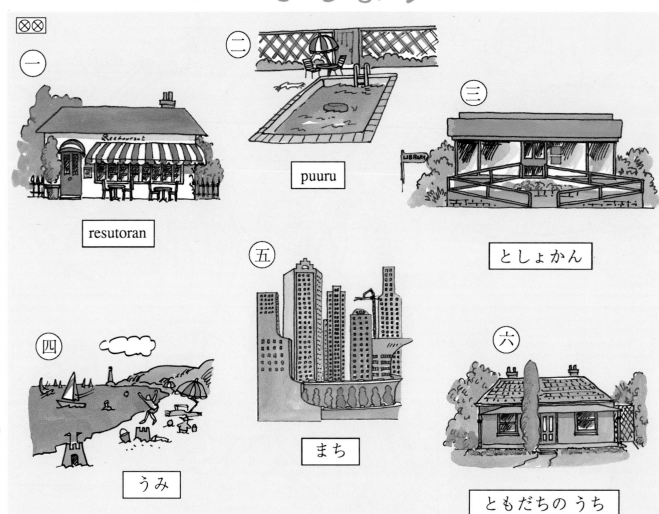

一　resutoran

二　puuru

三　としょかん

四　うみ

五　まち

六　ともだちの うち

Talk about the pictures using the example as a guide.

例:

A　きのう どこに いきましたか。
B　うみに いきました。

せんしゅう どこに いきましたか。　　　　Makudonarudoに いきました。

いいましょう 二

①

たのしかった です。

②

おいしかった です。

③

つまらなかった です。

④

あつかった です。

⑤

おかしかった です。

⑥

よかった です。

Talk about the pictures using the examples as a guide.

例:

A　Uiikuendoに どこに いきましたか。
B　まちに いきました。

例:

A　なにを しましたか。
B　かいものを しました。

例:

A　どう でしたか。
B　つまらなかった ですよ。

はなこさんと ゆうこさんの かぞく

あきら - 16
ただし - 45
えりこ - 41
まきこ - 65
としお - 10
ひでゆき - 70

Imagine that you are talking to Hanako and Yuuko about their family.
Use the examples as a guide.

例:

| A おばあさんの おなまえは? |
| B まきこ です。 |

例:

| A なんさいですか。 |
| B そぼは 六十五さい です。 |

かぞく		
はなこさんの...		わたしの...
おじいさん	grandfather	そふ
おばあさん	grandmother	そぼ
おとうさん	father	ちち
おかあさん	mother	はは
おにいさん	older brother	あに
おねえさん	older sister	あね
おとうとさん	younger brother	おとうと
いもうとさん	younger sister	いもうと

ともだちと

Make up a conversation with a partner. You have to decide who is A and who is B.

わたしは A です。

| A | Uiikuendoは どう でしたか。 |

ぼくは B です。

| B | よかった
たのしかった
つまらなかった | です。 |

| A | なにを しましたか。
どこに いきましたか。 |

| B | どようび
にちようび | に | sakkaa
かいもの
うみ
puuru | を
に | しました。
いきました。 |

| ただしくん、
みちこさん、
Kenくん、
Mandiiさん、 | uiikuendoは どう でしたか。 |

| A | よかった です。
あんまり... |

| きんようび
どようび
にちようび | の ごご | resutoran
ともだちのうち
としょかん
まち
おばあさんの うち | に | いきました。 |

| B | なに | を | しましたか。
たべましたか。
かいましたか。 |

| A | Piza
Teepu
ほん
えいが
Terebi | を | よみました。
たべました。
みました。
かいました。
ききました。 | おかしかった
おいしかった
つまらなかった
よかった
たのしかった | ですよ。 |

いきいきと はなしましょう

一 なにを しましたか。 どこに いきましたか。

How do your classmates spend their weekends?
Make a list of six things to do and four places to go at the weekend. Then ask five people in your class whether or not they did them or went there last weekend.

例:

Activities	1	2	3	4	5	total
かいものを しました						
おんがくを ききました						
tenisuを しました						
terebiを みました						
すいえいを しました						
まんがを よみました						
Places						
まちに いきました						
ともだちの うちに いきました						
としょかんに いきました						
うみに いきました						

What are the top three activities and places to go in your class?

二 Bring in some photos of your family and talk about them with a partner. You can talk about the following things.

・who they are, that is, what relation they are to you
・their name and age
・what things they like and dislike

Don't always wait for your friend to volunteer information, ask questions.

たんご

New words and expressions	
あたらしい	__ new
あつい	__ hot
あのね	__ hey!
いって	__ go!
きて	__ come!
きのう	__ yesterday
ごご	__ afternoon
すいえい	__ swimming
せんしゅう	__ last week
たのしい	__ fun, enjoyable
つまらない	__ boring
どう でしたか	__ what was it like?
とても	__ very
はいって	__ jump in!
ほんとう?	__ really?
また!	__ not again!
まって!	__ wait a minute!
みんな	__ everyone
やめて!	__ stop!

More past activities	
(を)かいました	__ bought
(に)いきました	__ went to

Places to go	
うみ	__ beach
こうえん	__ park
としょかん	__ library
ともだちの うち	__ friend's house
にわ	__ garden
puuru	__ swimming pool
まち	__ town
resutoran	__ restaurant

がんばれ!

Let's be flexible!

You will have realised by now that there are some expressions in Japanese that you cannot possibly understand by translating word-for-word. It just doesn't work!

For example, どうぞ roughly translates as *please* in English, but it has a whole range of meanings in Japanese depending on the context in which it is said. In Japanese you say どうぞ when you give someone something, but you wouldn't say *please* in English in this situation, would you? You would say something like *here you are* or *I've got something for you*.

Discovering new and different ways of expressing things is what makes learning a foreign language fun. You can learn a lot about the other culture in this way as well. For example, when a Japanese person answers the door and invites you in, they will most probably say, あがって ください. This expression literally means *come up, please*, but the real English equivalent is *come in, please*. Japanese people say *come up* because, as you know, before you go inside a Japanese house you go into the げんかん, where you take off your outside shoes. You then go up a step into the house.

All of this points to one thing - you have to be flexible when you are learning another language and not expect people from other countries to express themselves in exactly the same way as we English-speakers do. When it comes to expressions, in most cases it is better to learn them in context.

3-21, Yukinoshita 1-chome,
Kamakura-shi, Kanagawa-ken,
Japan

27th June

Hi everyone,

In this letter I'm going to tell you about our school trip to Kyoto and Nara and I'm not going to go off the point and start talking about baseball or anything. Except that, you know how I told you we won our first two games, well last week we played a really big match in the schools' regional championship. Well, it was really exciting, but we lost. All the girls were crying, everyone took it so seriously. I did too.

Except I just want to tell you about the pro game we went to the other night. It's called a 'naitaa'. It was in this huge new stadium, like a big egg-shell. I went with Mr Tanaka and Toshio. It was a great atmosphere at the game. Every time someone hit a 'hoomuran' they let off fireworks and the big screen on the scoreboard went beserk. It's funny hearing the umpire yelling out 'sutoraiki' and 'auto'. I think I've turned into a bit of a baseball fan since I've been here.

Anyway, I'd better get back to the school trip. It was at the end of May. That's the end of spring. I have to admit that it is really beautiful here in the spring. The countryside is all so green and the cherry blossoms are just great. I think I've turned into a baseball-loving nature freak.

Anyway, about the school trip! I was really looking forward to it because everyone else at school was so excited about it. My friend Eriko who likes to practise her English kept saying, 'I'm so exciting.' I went home and worked out what jeans and tops to take and then they told me that we wear our uniforms the whole time. Well, at least it saved on luggage.

Before the trip our teachers kept telling us how important Kyoto and Nara are in Japanese history. They keep saying that young people in Japan won't understand properly what it means to be Japanese if they ignore the past and just take notice of all the modern stuff around. In the olden days,

Kyoto was the capital of Japan for hundreds of years. The Emperor lived there and everything and he still gets crowned there. They told us that there were about 1,500 temples in Kyoto and I thought it could get a bit boring just going around looking at them all day. And Nara was the capital of Japan even before Kyoto. It's full of temples and shrines too.

Well, we got to the station early in the morning, and you should have seen us all. It wasn't just my class group, it was the whole of Year 2, eight classes of about 45, all at the station, waiting for the しんかんせん. You should have heard the noise. The teachers were running around with megaphones trying to get us organised and everyone was stocking up on junk-food to eat on the train.

We had a whole section of the train just for our school. Just as well, because no-one just sat in their seat. Everyone was so 'exciting', running around, sitting next to all different people and exploring the train. You could go up to the dining car and watch the digital readout of the train's speed. While I was watching it got up to 193 k.p.h. Someone said they saw it get up to 202 but I think they were just saying it.

Eriko started telling me about the envelopes of money that all of her family and friends had given her. Japanese people don't think it's nice to give you money unless it's in an envelope. Well, Eriko had about six envelopes, and she started planning what presents she was going to buy for all the people who gave her money. She told me I should start thinking about that too.

When I settled down and started looking out the window for a while I was amazed that we were still going through the suburbs of Tokyo. It seemed like we'd been going for ages, but the tall apartment buildings and the traffic and the expressways just kept going on and on and on. I listened to my walkman and stared out the window, and it was just more buildings, more motorways, more traffic. So I got up and went to talk to some of my friends.

When I came back to my window, things had changed. We were out in the countryside and everything was so green. They say that about half of Japan's farm land is used for growing rice and all the rice fields were this beautiful green colour. Anyway, you'd be watching this and all of a sudden you'd go into this long tunnel for a couple of minutes. Japan is really mountainous, and the train lines just cut right through the mountains. There must have been about thirty tunnels on the way - more, probably. And the train went along the coast too, so looking out the window didn't get boring.

One of our teachers was sitting near us and kept pointing out the castles that you could see up on the hillsides. I wasn't really expecting to see castles. They belonged to local samurai rulers called だいみょう. That was when the しょうぐん was really powerful in Japan.

きもの七

九十一

The train was sort of following the trail that the だいみょう used to take on the way up to Tokyo.

Oh no, I'm running out of space already. Look, I'll write again soon and tell you about the rest of the trip. And I won't mention baseball at all. Keep trying hard at your Japanese so that when you come over you'll have a really great time.

さようなら, everyone. By the way, I'd be happy with just a postcard from somebody!!! Hint, hint!!

Lots of love,

Simone xxx

日本語 nooto

一 Saying where you went

To find out where someone went, you ask,
どこに いきましたか。

Here are some examples of answers to this question.

e.g. うみに いきました。
I went to the beach.

みちこさんは せんしゅうの
どようびに paatiiに いきました。
Michiko went to a party last Saturday.

Notice that after どこ and the place where you went you need to say に.

二 Describing what something was like

おいしい です。	It is delicious.
おいしかった です。	It was delicious.
おかしい です。	It is funny.
おかしかった です。	It was funny.
いい です。	It is good.
よかった です。	It was good.

When you want to describe what something was like, you take off the final -い of the adjective and add -かった. This is the past form of adjectives.

Notice in the last pair of examples that いい becomes よかった.

三 My family and your family

In Japanese there are two words for each member of the family. Which one you use depends on whether you are talking about your family or someone else's family.

a) when you are talking about your family to someone else, you use the shorter words.

e.g. ははは すもうが だいすき です。
My mother really likes sumo wrestling.

それは いもうとの puuru です。
That's my little sister's pool.

ちちは aisukuriimuが だいすき です。
My father loves ice cream.

b) when you are talking about someone else's family, or addressing your own family, you use the longer, more polite words.

e.g. おとうとさんは sakkaaを しましたか。
Did your little brother play soccer?

おねえさんは なんさい ですか。
How is your older sister?

おとうさん、いって きます。
See you later, Dad.

おかあさん、きょう なにを しましたか。
What did you do today, Mum?

四 みんな or みなさん

Both of these words mean *everyone* when addressing a group of people. みんな is more casual than みなさん. So you only use it when you are talking to your friends. You should use みなさん with people whom you don't know very well or who are older than you.

おめでとう！

Now you can do all of the following things in Japanese.

· talk about where you went
· ask someone about the weekend
· say what your own weekend was like
· comment on what something was like
· tell a story about what someone else did
· ask about someone else's family
· talk about your own family

らいしゅう から なつやすみ ですね。
みなさん、なつやすみ に なにを しますか。
はなこさんは? ゆうこさんは?

ええと、ちちと ははと あにと
おとうとと 日本に いきます。

ああ、そう ですか。いい ですね。
いつ いきますか。

らいしゅうの かようびに いきます。

ああ! きょうとに
しんかんせんで いきますか。

とうきょう tawaaに
いきますか。

ふじさんを
みますか。

みなさん、ちょっと まって!
ゆうこさん、とうきょうに
いきますか。

ええ、とうきょうに
いきます。

ええ、たぶん。

じゃ、ぎんざに
いきますか。
かいものを しますか。

みなさん、くうこうに
いきましょうか。

そう ですね。はなこさん、ひこうきは
なんじに でますか。

四じに でます。

じゃ、みなさん、一じはんに
あいましょう。

かようび です。

いま なんじ ですか。

一じ です。

Hanbaagaaを たべましょうか。

ええ、たべましょう。

でも...一じはんに せんせいに あいますね。おくれますよ。

いいえ、だいじょうぶ。Jianguくん、きて!

ああ、おいしい!

Hoseくん、いそいで ください。おくれますよ。

ああー!

だいじょうぶ。つぎの basuで いきましょう。

いいましょう一

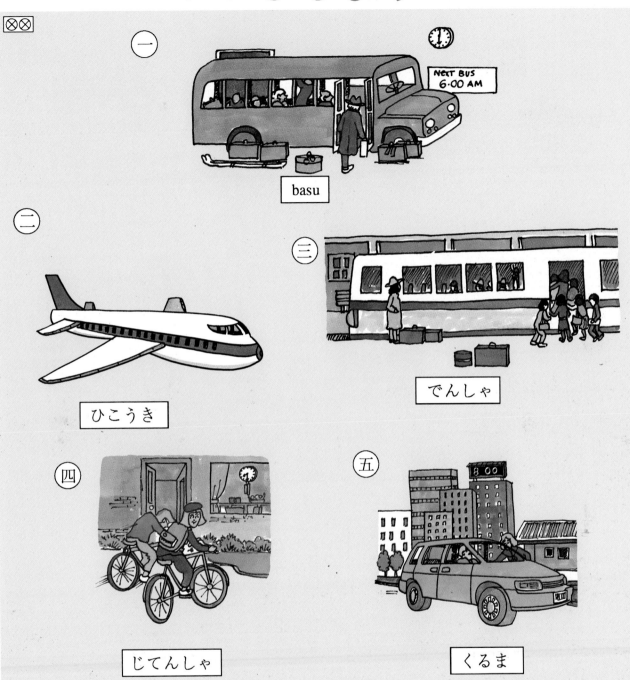

一 basu

二 ひこうき

三 でんしゃ

四 じてんしゃ

五 くるま

Talk about the pictures using the example as a guide.

例:

A ひこうきで いきますか。
B はい、ひこうきで いきます。
　 or
　 いいえ、でんしゃで いきます。

いいましょう 二

一　すいえい

二　じょうば

三　さんぽ

四　saikuringu

Talk about the pictures using the examples as a guide.

例:

A あした なにを しますか。
B じょうばを します。

例:

A なんじに しますか。
B 十二じに します。

あした なにを しますか。

さんぽを します。

いいましょう 三

一　うみ

二　resutoran

三　kyanpu

四　やきゅうの geemu

五　やま

Talk about the pictures using the examples as a guide.

例:

| A　どこに いきましょうか。 |
| B　やまに いきましょう。 |

例:

| A　Kyanpuに いきましょうか。 |
| B　ええ、いきましょう。 |

ともだちと

Make up a conversation with a partner. You have to decide who is A and who is B.

A	もしもし。

B	もしもし。	ひろし まきこ	です。	ひでくん、 えりこさん、	あした なにを しますか。

A	しゅくだい Terebi まんが	を	します。 よみます。 みます。

B	つまらない ですよ。	うみ まち としおくんの うち	に	いきましょうか。

A	そう? なにを しますか。

B	すいえい えいが かいもの Geemu おんがく	を	します。 みます。 ききます。

A	いい ですね。	Basu でんしゃ じてんしゃ	で	いきましょうか。

B	ええ、 いいえ、	basu でんしゃ じてんしゃ	で	いきましょう。

A	なんじに あいましょうか。

B	十じはん 二じ 十二じはん	に	あいましょう。じゃあね。

A	じゃまたね。

いきいきと はなしましょう

It's the summer holidays and you and your friend are spending a week at a holiday camp in the country.

Every day the organisers of the camp put out a programme of activities that you can do that day. Today's programme is reproduced below.

At each time you can choose between two activities. With your friend, plan what you are going to do today, taking it in turns to make suggestions.
On a separate piece of paper draw up a programme like the one below, and next to each time write in Japanese what you have decided to do.

じかん		
9.00		
10.30		
12.00		
1.30		
3.00		
4.30		
6.00		
7.30		

Now compare your programme with someone else's and discuss what you are going to do at each time. As you are doing this try to make use of as much as possible of the language you have learned this year. You might want to comment on the other person's choice by saying things like,

おりがみは つまらない です。わたしは baree booru を します。

or

わたしも！ けんどうは たのしい ですね。

And don't forget to use all those little 'filler' expressions like ええと, じゃ, さあ that make your conversation sound really Japanese.

せいかつ

3-21, Yukinoshita 1-chome,
Kamakura-shi, Kanagawa-ken,
Japan

12th July

Hi everyone,

I am really going to finish telling you about the school trip - and no talking about how we won our last game and Scott hit a 'hoomuran' or anything. Except...no!!!

Well, in my last letter we were all on the train heading for Kyoto and I was looking out the window and this teacher was telling us some historical stuff about the castles and that. Anyway, while this was going on, people started saying, 'ふじさん, ふじさん.' That meant we were getting near Mt Fuji so I grabbed my camera and went to get a window spot on the right side of the train. Then everyone started saying, 'There it is!' but I couldn't see it and kept saying,'Where, where?' Then the teacher told me to look up really high, and there it was. It was really great, just like all the postcards I'd seen, so I took about ten shots of it - more, probably. It's a really nice looking volcano. You don't think much about Japan being a country of volcanoes and earthquakes while you're here.

Well, Kyoto turned out to be really interesting. We went around to all these different temples and things trying not to lose sight of our 'gaidosan' who carried a flag with our school emblem and a number on it. She would be up the front telling us all the historical details about the places we visited, but no-one was listening. All the kids kept looking out for foreigners (がいじん) and calling out 'haroo' to them and making peace signs.

My favourite place in Kyoto was Ryoanji temple. Well, it wasn't actually the temple, but the rock garden they have there. What it is, is these 15 rocks arranged in this special sort of way in a gravel courtyard. I know it doesn't sound exciting, but it was just so still and sort of perfect. There was no rubbish or anything. You were supposed to go in there and just look at the garden and meditate. When we got there Eriko said, 'Is that all it is?' and went off to look for more

がいじん and buy some souvenirs. I really wanted to try to meditate in the garden but the others kept hurrying me up and getting me to pose in their photographs. The cameras never stopped clicking and I must have been in about fifty different group shots - more, probably.

We also went to the きんかくじ (Golden Pavilion). I sort of tagged onto this group of American tourists and I heard their guide say that it belonged to a powerful しょうぐん hundreds of years ago. Then it was turned into a Zen temple after he died. What I liked was the way it was reflected in the water. It was like looking at two temples. Just to show how rich he was the しょうぐん had the walls sort of coated in this 24 carat gold. One of the tourists asked how much it would be worth in U.S. dollars but the guide just smiled. I don't think he knew.

The best part of the whole trip was going out at night. We were allowed to go into town to do some shopping and teachers didn't come or anything. We still had to wear our uniform but I was getting used to that. We were just sort of trusted not to go to coffee shops or other places that are banned. Kyoto is not just temples, it's also a really modern city with fantastic shopping arcades.

We slept at an inn in Kyoto. We were in these really big rooms with about 15 people in it - more, probably. There wasn't much room on the floor when we all spread out our ふとん on the たたみ mats to go to sleep. Japanese inns give you these pillows full of beans to sleep on and I found it really hard to get comfortable on them. They made an awful racket every time you moved your head. So, what with all the giggling and that, it was pretty hard to get to sleep the first night. The second night I put the pillow under the ふとん.

Our second day was spent at Nara, the very earliest capital of Japan. It looked a bit different from Kyoto. I can remember these really old wooden houses in the some of the streets. But the main thing at Nara is Todaiji Temple. It's actually a lot of different sorts of temples in this huge park. To get into it you go under this really big old wooden front gate. I heard our 'gaidosan' say that the original one was blown down by a typhoon in the olden days. I haven't seen any typhoons yet, but everyone says just wait until September!

The most famous part of the Todaiji Temple is the だいぶつでん. It's the biggest wooden

building in the world and inside is this absolutely huge Buddha. What surprised me was with all the noise our school was making and all the cameras flashing and everything, the Buddha kept this really peaceful look on his face.

The other good thing at Nara was going for a walk in the deer park which was all around the Todaiji Temple. The deer were really tame and you could buy special biscuits to feed them. I was going to buy some but they were a bit too deer. Get it? Anyway, they looked pretty well fed, and I thought they were a bit smelly.

Well, that was our school trip. That was a few weeks ago. Now the rainy season (つゆ) has started, that's how come I'm staying inside and catching up with some letter writing. Well, I'm not going out in that, it's just drizzles all the time. At least it's not cold. Mr and Mrs Tanaka bought me matching umbrella and gumboots for つゆ. They're bright yellow with a red pattern on them. I feel really stupid in these short rubber boots, but everyone is wearing them. And as for umbrellas, well, there are about 120 million people in Japan, and that's about how many umbrellas there are too.

Well, I've run out of news and space. Thanks for your letters. At last!!! Yes, I am still doing けんどう, no, I don't have a photo of Scott to send, yes, I do miss being home sometimes. Must dash.

Love to everyone,

Simone xxxxx

日本語 *nooto*

一 Saying what you are going to do

Uiikuendoに なにを しますか。
What are you going to do at the weekend?

こうえんに いきます。
I'm going to the park.

ゆうこさんは? じょうばを します。
And Yuuko? She's going horse riding.

Notice that all of the verbs at the end of the sentence end in -ます. This part of the verb indicates that you are *going to do* something.

二 Let's...

Pizaを たべましょうか。
Shall we have a pizza.

ええ、たべましょう。
Yes, let's.

あつい ですね。
Puuruに いきましょうか。
It's hot, isn't it? Let's go to the pool.

When you want to suggest doing something, you use the -ましょうか ending on the verbs.

三 At what time...?

To ask or tell *at* what time something is happening, you use に.

e.g. 一じはんに hanbaagaaを
たべました。
I ate a hamburger at half past one.

なんじに あいましょうか。
(At) what time shall we meet?

Even though you don't have to say *at* when asking the question in English, you must always say に in Japanese.

四 に

We have now seen three different meanings of に.

a) It can mean *to*, when talking about going or coming to a place.

e.g. 日本に いきます。
I'm going to Japan.

どこに いきましたか。
Where did you go?

わたしの うちに きて。
Come to my house!

b) It can mean *at* or *on* with the time, the days of the week and *uiikuendo*.

e.g. 二じに さんぽを しました。
I went for a walk at 2 o'clock.

にちようびに うみに いきました。
I went to the beach on Sunday.

Uiikuendoに なにを しましたか。
What did you do at the weekend?

c) It is used when talking about meeting someone

e.g. 一じはんに せんせいに
あいますね。
We're meeting the teacher at 1.30, aren't we?

ともだちに あいました。
それから、puuruに いきました。
I met a friend. And then we went to the pool.

五 で meaning *by*

To say that you went *by* bus, bike etc., you say で after the mode of transport.

e.g. じてんしゃで いきました。
I went by bike.

でんしゃで いきましょうか。
Shall we go by train?

Basuで まちに いきました。
We went to the city by bus.

Notice the word order in the last example, where the place is mentioned as well.

六 と meaning *with*

おとうとと terebiを みました。
I watched television with my little brother.

あねと tenisuを しました。
I played tennis with my big sister.

きもの 八 ● 百四

七 Summary of Japanese verbs

This table is a summary of the verbs you have learned so far.

	did...	going to...	let's...
meet	あいました	あいます	あいましょう
go	いきました	いきます	いきましょう
buy	かいました	かいます	かいましょう
listen (to)	ききました	ききます	ききましょう
do, play	しました	します	しましょう
eat	たべました	たべます	たべましょう
drink	のみました	のみます	のみましょう
watch, look, see	みました	みます	みましょう
read	よみました	よみます	よみましょう

たんご

New words and expressions	
あした — tomorrow	だいじょうぶ — don't worry, it's O.K.
(に)あいます — meet, going to meet	たぶん — perhaps
いそいで ください — hurry up, please	でます — leave, going to leave
おくれます — be late, going to be late	...と — with..., and
から — from	つぎ — the next
kyanpu — camping	で — by
くうこう — airport	なつやすみ — summer holiday
saikuringu — cycling	やま — mountain
さんぽ — a walk	らいしゅう — next week
じゃ — well then...	らいねん — next year
じょうば — horse riding	

おめでとう!

Now you can do all of the following things in Japanese.

· talk about where you are going to go and what you are going to do
· ask others what they are going to do
· ask and say at what time something is happening
· say how you are going to travel
· make suggestions on what to do

Appendix

すうじ

一	1	いち
二	2	に
三	3	さん
四	4	よん or し
五	5	ご
六	6	ろく
七	7	なな or しち
八	8	はち
九	9	きゅう or く
十	10	じゅう
十一	11	じゅういち
十二	12	じゅうに
十三	13	じゅうさん
十四	14	じゅうよん or じゅうし
十五	15	じゅうご
十六	16	じゅうろく
十七	17	じゅうしち or じゅうなな
十八	18	じゅうはち
十九	19	じゅうきゅう
二十	20	にじゅう
二十一	21	にじゅういち
二十二	22	にじゅうに
三十	30	さんじゅう
三十五	35	さんじゅうご
四十	40	よんじゅう
五十	50	ごじゅう
六十	60	ろくじゅう
七十	70	ななじゅう or しちじゅう
八十	80	はちじゅう
八十一	81	はちじゅういち
八十八	88	はちじゅうはち
九十	90	きゅうじゅう
九十九	99	きゅうじゅうきゅう
百	100	ひゃく

...さい

1	一さい	（いっさい）
2	二さい	
3	三さい	
4	四さい	（よんさい）
5	五さい	
6	六さい	
7	七さい	（ななさい）
8	八さい	（はっさい）
9	九さい	（きゅうさい）
10	十さい	（じゅっさい）
11	十一さい	（じゅういっさい）
12	十二さい	
13	十三さい	
14	十四さい	（じゅうよんさい）
15	十五さい	
16	十六さい	
17	十七さい	（じゅうななさい）
18	十八さい	（じゅうはっさい）
19	十九さい	（じゅうきゅうさい）
20	はたち	
21	二十一さい	（にじゅういっさい）

つき（月）

January	一がつ
February	二がつ
March	三がつ
April	四がつ （しがつ）
May	五がつ
June	六がつ
July	七がつ （しちがつ）
August	八がつ
September	九がつ （くがつ）
October	十がつ
November	十一がつ
December	十二がつ

...じ

1 o'clock	一じ
2 o'clock	二じ
3 o'clock	三じ
4 o'clock	四じ （よじ）
5 o'clock	五じ
6 o'clock	六じ
7 o'clock	七じ （しちじ）
8 o'clock	八じ
9 o'clock	九じ （くじ）
10 o'clock	十じ
11 o'clock	十一じ
12 o'clock	十二じ

...ばん

1st	一ばん
2nd	二ばん
3rd	三ばん
4th	四ばん （よんばん）
5th	五ばん
6th	六ばん
7th	七ばん
8th	八ばん
9th	九ばん
10th	十ばん

たんご 日本語 - 英語

あ

ああ、あっ!	oh! ah!
ああ、おいしい	yum!
ああ、そう	ah, I see
aisukuriimu	ice cream
あいます	meet
あかちゃん	baby
あがって ください	come in!
あけて	open it!
あした	tomorrow
あたらしい	new
あつい	hot
あなた	you
あに	(my) older brother
あね	(my) older sister
あのね	hey!
あひる	duck
あぶない	dangerous
あぶなく ない です	it's not dangerous
ありがとう	thanks
ありがとうございます	thank you
あれ!	look! heavens above!
あんまり	
いいえ、あんまり…	I don't really (like it)

い

いい	good
いい おてんき ですね	it's nice weather, isn't it?
いいえ	no, don't mention it
いきます	go
いそいで	hurry!
いただきます	expression used before eating
いつ	when
いって	go!
いってきます	goodbye (used by person leaving)
いってらっしゃい	goodbye (used by person remaining)
いま	now
いもうと(さん)	little sister
いぬ	dog
いのしし	wild boar

う

uiikuendo	weekend
うさぎ	rabbit
うし	cow
うた	song
うち	house
うちわ	Japanese fan
うま	horse
うみ	sea, beach
うるさい	noisy, loud, annoying

え

え、えっ!?	what's this!?
えっ、なに?	what did you say?
えいご(英語)	English
ええ	yes, yeah
ええと	well then, let's see
えき	railway station
えんぴつ	pencil

お

おいしい	delicious
おおきい	big
おかあさん	mother, Mum
おかし	sweet, lolly
おかしい	funny
おくれます	be late
おすし	sushi
おそい	late
おそく なって すみません	I'm sorry I'm late
おちゃ	green tea
おてんき	weather
おとうさん	father, Dad
おとうと(さん)	little brother
おばあさん	old lady, grandmother
おはよう	good morning
おはようございます	good morning
おなまえ	name
おなまえは?	what's your name?
おにいさん	older brother
おねえさん	older sister
おやおや	oh dear! really!
おやすみなさい	goodnight
orenji juusu	orange juice
おんがく	music

か

…か	…?
かいます	buy
かいもの	shopping
かえる	frog
かがく	science
かして	lend!
がっこう	school
かようび	Tuesday
から	from
からて	karate
karee raisu	curry and rice
かわいい	cute, pretty
がんばれ	come on!

き

きいて	listen!
ききます	listen (to); hear
きたない	dirty, untidy
きって	stamp
きっぷ	ticket
きて	come!
きのう	yesterday
きみ	you (men and boys only)
kyanpu	camping
きょう	today
きょうだい	brothers and sisters
きんようび	Friday

く

くうこう	airport

ください	please
きいて ください	listen, please
くるま	car
くん	form of address (boys)

け

keeki	cake
geemu	game
けしgomu	eraser
げつようび	Monday
けんどう	kendo (Japanese fencing)

こ

こいのぼり	Japanese carp kite
こうえん	park
kooto	coat
koohii	coffee
koora	coke
こくばん	blackboard
ごご	afternoon
kotsu kotsu	knock knock
ごはん	bowl of rice
これ(は)	this
こんにちは	hello, good afternoon
こんばんは	good evening

さ

さあ	um... (I don't know)
...さい	...years old
saikuringu	cycling
sakkaa	soccer
ざっし	magazine
さようなら	goodbye
さる	monkey
さん	form of address
さんぽ	a walk
さんぽを します	go for a walk

し

...じ	...o'clock
四じ です	it's four o'clock
じかん	time, hour
じかん です	it's time to go
じかんひょう	timetable

じてんしゃ	bicycle
します	do, play (sport, games)
しめて	close it!
じゃ	well then...
じゃ あとで	see you soon
じゃ あね	see you soon
しゃかい	social studies
じゃまたね	see you later
じゅうしょ	address
しゅくだい	homework
じょうず	good (at something)
じょうば	horse riding
しんかんせん	Shinkansen (bullet train)

す

すいえい	swimming
すいえいを します	to swim, go swimming
すいようび	Wednesday
すうがく	maths
すき	like (something)
sukeeto boodo	skateboard
すごい	great, fantastic
supagetti	spaghetti
supootsu	sport
すみません	excuse me, I'm sorry
すもう	sumo wrestling
すわって	sit down!

せ

せんしゅう	last week
せんせい	teacher

そ

そう	
そう ですね	I agree
それ(は)	that
それから	then, after that
そふ	grandfather
そば	grandmother

た

たいいく	phys. ed.
だいじょうぶ	don't worry

だいすき	like (something) a lot
たつ	dragon
たって	stand up!
たのしい	fun, enjoyable
たぶん	perhaps, maybe
たべます	eat
tawaa	tower
たんじょうび	birthday
たんじょうび おめでとう!	happy birthday!

ち

ちいさい	small
ちち	father, (my) dad
ちょうちん	Japanese lantern
ちょっと	a little
ちょっと まって	wait a moment!

つ

つき	moon
つぎ	the next one
つまらない	boring

て

で	by
じてんしゃで	by bike
teepu	tape
です	am, are, is
tenisu	tennis
でます	leave
でも	but
terebi	television
でんしゃ	train
でんわ	telephone
でんわ ばんごう	telephone number

と

と	with, and
doa	door
どう	
どう したん ですか	what happened?
どう でしたか	what was it like?
どうぞ	please, take it

どうぞよろしく pleased to meet you
とおり street
どこ where
としょかん library
とても very
ともだち friend
どようび Saturday
とら tiger
とり bird

な

なつ summer
　なつやすみ summer holiday
なに (なん) what
　なにどし which year sign were you born under?
　なんさい how old?
　なんばん what number?
(お)なまえ name

に

にちようび Sunday
にほんご (日本語) Japanese
にわ garden
にんぎょう doll

ね

ね ...isn't it
ねこ cat
ねずみ mouse, rat
ねんれい age

の

の of, possessive
　わたしの my
のみます drink

は

paatii party
はい yes
はいって jump in!
bai bai bye, bye
basu bus
はは mother, (my) mum
はやい early

はる spring
baree booru volleyball
…ばん number...
ばんごう number
hanbaagaa hamburger

ひ

ひ day
ひこうき aeroplane
piza pizza
ひつじ sheep

ふ

puuru swimming pool
ふじさん Mt Fuji
ふでばこ pencil-case
purezento present

へ

へええ! huh!
へび snake
pen pen

ほ

ほく I (men and boys)
ほし star
hotto doggu hot dog
ほん book
ほんとう? really?

ま

まずい (tastes) awful
まち town
また again
　また! not again!
またね see you soon
まって wait!
まど window
まんが comic

み

みて look!
みなさん everyone
みます see, watch, look at
miruku milk
みんな everyone

む

むずかしい difficult

も

も too, also
　わたしも me too
もくようび Thursday
もしもし hello (on the telephone)
ものさし ruler

や

やきそば Japanese fried noodles
やきゅう baseball
やさしい easy
やま mountain
やめて stop it!/that!

よ

よかった
　よかった です it was good
よみます read

ら

らいしゅう next week
らいねん next year

れ

れきし history
resutoran restaurant

わ

わあ! ahhh!
わかりました I understand, understood
わかりません I don't understand
わたし I
　わたしの my
　わたしも me too

A

aeroplane	ひこうき
address	じゅうしょ
afternoon	ごご
again	また
ah, I see	ああ、そう
airport	くうこう
am, are, is	です
and	と
awful (tastes)	まずい

B

baseball	やきゅう
bicycle	じてんしゃ
big	おおきい
bird	とり
birthday	たんじょうび
happy birthday!	たんじょうび おめでとう!
blackboard	こくばん
book	ほん
boring	つまらない
brother	
older	おにいさん, あに
younger	おとうとさん, おとうと
bus	basu
buy	かいます
but	でも
by	で
bye	じゃ またね, じゃあね, bai bai

C

cake	keeki
camping	kyanpu
car	くるま
cat	ねこ
chopsticks	おはし
close it	しめて ください
coat	kooto
coffee	koohii
coke	koora
come!	きて ください
come in!	どうぞ あがって ください
come on!	がんばれ!
comic	まんが
cow	うし
curry	karee raisu
cute, pretty	かわいい
cycling	saikuringu

D

dangerous	あぶない
not dangerous	あぶなく ない
day	ひ
delicious	おいしい
difficult	むずかしい
dirty, untidy	きたない
do	します
dog	いぬ
door	doa
dragon	たつ
drink	のみます
duck	あひる

E

early	はやい
easy	やさしい
eat	たべます
English	えいご (英語)
eraser	けしgomu
everyone	みなさん, みんな
excuse me, I'm sorry	すみません

F

father, Dad	ちち, おとうさん
fantastic	すごい
Friday	きんようび
friend	ともだち
frog	かえる
from	から
fun, enjoyable	たのしい
funny	おかしい

G

game	geemu
garden	にわ
go	いきます
go!	いって ください
good	いい
good (at something)	じょうず
goodbye	さようなら
good evening	こんばんは
good morning	おはよう (ございます)
goodnight	おやすみ なさい
grandfather	おじいさん, そふ
grandmother	おばあさん, そば
great, fantastic	すごい
gymnastics	たいいく

H

hamburger	hanbaagaa
happy birthday!	たんじょうび おめでとう!
hello (on the telephone)	もしもし
hello, good afternoon	こんにちは
here	
here, take it	どうぞ
hey!	あのね
history	れきし
holidays	おやすみ
summer holidays	なつやすみ
homework	しゅくだい
horse	うま
horse riding	じょうば
hot	あつい
hot dog	hotto doggu
house	うち
how	
how old are you?	なんさい ですか
hurry!	いそいで ください

I

I	わたし
I (men and boys)	ぼく
ice cream	aisukuriimu
...isn't it?	...ね
it is	です

J

Japanese	にほんご (日本語)
jump in! (in the pool)	はいって ください

K

karate	からて
kendo (Japanese fencing)	けんどう

L

last week	せんしゅう
late	
be late	おくれます
I'm sorry, I'm late	おそく なって すみません
leave	でます
lend	かして ください
library	としょかん
like (something)	すき
like (something) a lot	だいすき
listen	きいて ください
listen (to), hear	ききます
little	ちいさい
look	みて ください
look! heavens!	あれ!
look (at)	みます

M

maths	すうがく
maybe	たぶん
meet	あいます
milk	miruku
Monday	げつようび
monkey	さる
mother, Mum	はは, おかあさん
mountain	やま
mouse	ねずみ
music	おんがく
my	わたしの, ぼくの(men and boys)

N

name	(お)なまえ
what's your name?	おなまえは?
new	あたらしい
next	つぎ
next week	らいしゅう
next year	らいねん
no	いいえ
noisy, loud, annoying	うるさい
now	いま
number...	...ばん

O

...o'clock	...じ
O.K.	
it's O.K.	だいじょうぶ
of	の
oh dear! really!	おやおや
oh! ah!	あっ! あ!
old lady, grandmother	おばあさん
open	あけて ください
orange juice	orenji juusu

P

park	こうえん
party	paatii
pen	pen
pencil	えんぴつ
pencil-case	ふでばこ
perhaps	たぶん
phys. ed.	たいいく
pizza	piza
play (sport, game)	します
please	どうぞ
pleased to meet you	どうぞ よろしく
pool	puuru
present	purezento

R

rabbit	うさぎ
rat	ねずみ
read	よみます
really?	ほんとう
restaurant	resutoran
ruler	ものさし

S

Saturday	どようび
school	がっこう
science	かがく
sea, beach	うみ
see, watch	みます
I see, I understand	ああ、そう、そう ですね、わかりました
see you later	じゃ またね、じゃ あとで、じゃあね
see you next year	また らいねん
sheep	ひつじ
shopping	かいもの
I'm going shopping	かいものを します
sister	
older	おねえさん, あね
younger	いもうとさん, いもうと
sit down	すわって ください
skateboard	sukeeto boodo

きもの たんご ● 百十一

small	ちいさい
snake	へび
soccer	sakkaa
social studies	しゃかい
song	うた
spaghetti	supagetti
sport	supootsu
spring	はる
stand up!	たって ください
stop it!	やめて ください
summer	なつ
summer holidays	なつやすみ
sumo wrestling	すもう
Sunday	にちようび
sushi	おすし
sweet, lolly	おかし
swimming	すいえい
I went swimming	すいえいを しました
swimming pool	puuru

T

tape	teepu
tea (green tea)	おちゃ
teacher	せんせい
telephone	でんわ
telephone number	でんわ ばんごう
television	terebi
tennis	tenisu
thank you	ありがとう
that	それ(は)
then, after that	それから
this	これ (は)
tiger	とら
timetable	じかんひょう
today	きょう
tomorrow	あした
too, also	も
town	まち
train	でんしゃ
Thursday	もくようび
Tuesday	かようび

U

understand	
I understand	わかりました
I don't understand	わかりません

V

very	とても
volleyball	baree booru

W

wait!	まって ください
wait a moment!	ちょっと まって
walk	さんぽ
go for a walk	さんぽを します
weather	おてんき
it's nice weather, isn't it	いい おてんき ですね
Wednesday	すいようび
weekend	uiikuendo
well...	じゃ
well then, let's see	ええと
what	なん, なに
what happened?	どう したん ですか
what number?	なんばん
what was it like?	どう でしたか
when	いつ
where	どこ
wild boar	いのしし
window	まど
with	と
worry	
don't worry	だいじょうぶ

Y

year	
...years old	...さい
yes	はい
yes, yeah	ええ
yesterday	きのう
yum!	ああ、おいしい